DYSLEXIA
AND OTHER LEARNING DIFFICULTIES

The Essential Guide

Maria Chivers

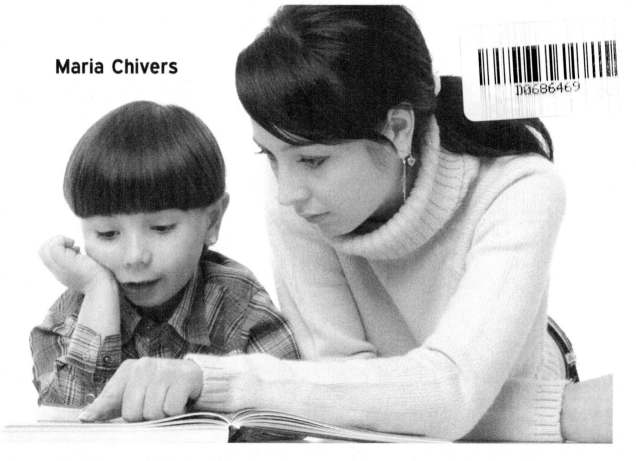

Dyslexia – A Parent's Guide is also available in accessible formats for people with any degree of visual impairment. The large print edition and eBook (with accessibility features enabled) are available from Need2Know. Please let us know if there are any special features you require and we will do our best to accommodate your needs.

First published in Great Britain in 2011 by
Need2Know
Remus House
Coltsfoot Drive
Peterborough
PE2 9BF
Telephone 01733 898103
Fax 01733 313524
www.need2knowbooks.co.uk

Contents

Contributors

Dr David Cowell

B.Sc. M.Phil. Ph.D. Dip Psych.

David Cowell trained as a psychologist at the Tavistock Centre, London, before moving to work in the North of England. He was senior psychologist in Swindon for 18 years, but is now an independent consultant specialising in child and adolescent problems. He has an M.Phil. and Ph.D. from Exeter University and has written or contributed to a number of books. He has participated in many radio and television programmes.

Dr Richard Eyre

Consultant in Child and Adolescent Psychiatry

Dr Richard Eyre is a member of the Royal College of Psychiatrists and used to be a consultant in Child and Adolescent Psychiatry at Princess Margaret Hospital in Swindon. Having completed higher training at the Maudsley and King's College Hospitals, he developed interests in adolescent psychiatry and family therapy. As a consultant psychiatrist in Richmond (1991-94), he worked closely with the Local Authority's Social Services Department and Education Department in developing inter-agency approaches to child protection issues and children with educational difficulties associated with school-based problems such as poor behaviour and attendance. When he was in Swindon he was responsible particularly for special services for children under the age of eight.

Keith Holland

B.Sc. FBCO. DCLP.

Keith is an optometrist practising in Cheltenham, Gloucestershire, with a special interest in vision and learning. Over the last 20 years he has built up one of the largest specialist practices in Europe, dealing with the visual problems associated with dyslexia and learning difficulties. His practice has twice been awarded the title 'Specialist Eye Care Practice of the Year' and also 'The Children's Eye Care Practice of the Year'. Keith has published many articles on the links between vision and literacy, and lectures widely on the subject, both at home and abroad. He is founder and chairman of the British Association of Behavioural Optometrists, a professional special interest group that represents practitioners around Britain working in this field. He is married and has four children.

Christine Robinson (nee Mann)
DBO. SRO.

Christine was born and educated in Birmingham, England. She trained as an orthoptist at the Children's Hospital, Birmingham, and worked from 1964 at the Princess Margaret Hospital, Swindon, recently transferring to the new Great Western Way Hospital, Swindon. Christine is married and has three sons, two of whom are dyslexic. She has had an interest in dyslexia for the last 20 years and enjoys assessing and helping children who are dyslexic. It is very useful to be able to see the problems from two different perspectives – a parent of dyslexic children and as a professional who is able to advise and treat.

A note of thanks

I would like to express my thanks to all the staff at the Swindon Dyslexia Centre, in particular to Deirdre Holland who inspired me many years ago, and for their continued help and support not just in preparing this book, but for the help with running the centre.

Special thanks are also extended to the specialists who have contributed to this book:

Dr D Cowell B.Sc. M.Phil. Ph.D. Dip. Psych.

Dr R Eyre – consultant in Child and Adolescent Psychiatry.

Keith Holland B.Sc, FBCO, DCLP.

Christine Robinson DBO, SRO.

The British Dyslexia Association.

Disclaimer

This book is for general information about dyslexia and other learning difficulties. It is not intended to replace professional medical advice. It can be used alongside medical advice, but anyone concerned about their child is strongly advised to consult their GP.

I'm Not Marking This Mess

I can see his face ready to blow
he shouts so the whole class will know
'Sir, Sir I'm stuck, I need more time.'
'I told you what to do, don't step out of line.'

I find it hard and embarrassing with him yelling
about my reading, writing and spelling.
'Hurry up, get on with it, I'm not marking this mess.'
I say, 'I need more time, I'm doing my best.'

He tells me little kids can do better than me
'I've seen better from my daughter, she's only three
where's your full stops and capital letters?
Now go and sit down until you do better.'

It's hard to do my work I find
I never rest, it's always on my mind
then I get frustrated, rude and angry
because he doesn't understand me.

By Mark Chivers (12)
September 1995.

Reprinted by kind persmission of *The Inner Hurt*.

Introduction

'Please teacher,
if I can't learn by the way you teach,
please teach me the way I learn'

Extract from a poem

Millions of children go to school. The majority get along in the educational system with no problems. However, for some children who have special needs, it appears to be the start of an ongoing battle. These children usually need special education which often takes years to identify and costs a great deal of money.

Parents, particularly mothers, feel a sense of loss when their children first start school. Most children are also anxious but then the eagerness to absorb the wonders of school and all the avenues that open up comes into being. Sadly, for some parents a few months later, their dreams and aspirations are shattered. Their children do not seem to be on the same level with other children in class. Their classmates seem to be racing ahead.

Waiting for your child after school each afternoon seems fraught with problems. As the other children come pouring into the playground, clutching their reading folders, your child throws his arms around you for a hug and you hear the other mothers saying 'Another new book today, how wonderful.' Looking at your child's folder, you realise that your child is still on the same one. You try not to show your disappointment because you are fully aware that intelligence is not based only on reading. (But try telling the other mothers that!)

For several years you are encased in a vicious circle. Teachers appear to take it personally when your child does not read or write along with his peers. As with anything, it may take one child several years to read and another just a few weeks. Some children actually go to school reading.

'This book is dedicated to the hundreds of thousands of parents who battle every day with bureaucracy to get equal rights for their children in schools.'

Please note: for ease of reading he should be transposed for she when appropriate.

I have also talked about mothers rather than fathers because the vast majority of parents having the most dealings with young children are still their mothers.

After your child has been at school for a short time, this difference can be very clearly seen. Parents continue to voice their concerns to the class teacher, only to be fobbed off with, 'He'll catch up.' The longer it goes on, the worse it gets. Relationships with teachers deteriorate, until in the end it seems like a constant battle of us and them. The teachers label you as 'troublesome' or 'overanxious' parents and, as the relationship continues to crumble, your child senses this anxiety. Many parents who find themselves in this position say that school is a battlefield.

Some of the reasons for your child falling behind at school can include difficulty with:

- Reading, writing or number work.
- Speaking, hearing or sight.
- A physical or mental disability.
- Emotional or behavioural problems.
- Medical or health problems.

'Teachers appear to take it personally when your child does not read or write along with his peers.'

You may, as parents, be asking yourselves where you can go for help and what your legal rights are. Throughout the country there are many organisations and publications that exist to help parents – but do you know where to find them?

Parents are often at the end of their tether when they call for help. In many cases if they asked for advice from the right people earlier, the problems could have been sorted out much more quickly. These difficulties often result in great frustration, not only for parents and teachers but also for the child, who falls even further behind and loses more self-esteem with each day.

This book is written in an easy-to-follow format. It aims to point you in the right direction in order to get the appropriate help and support in the quickest possible time, avoiding the sense of failure for your child and the pain and frustration for you, the parents.

Chapter One

I Know There is Something Wrong – But No One Will Listen!

Every mother knows when there is something wrong with her child. This happened to me when my eldest son, Jeremy, started school. It is extremely frustrating to be told that the child is just naughty, lazy, slow or will not listen. Many of these children are desperately unhappy as they go through their school life being at the bottom of the class, knowing the answers but never being able to put them on paper.

Within a few months of Jeremy starting school, I started to talk to his teacher about his slow progress. I knew he was not learning at the same pace as the other children in his group. His friends would be reading different books almost every day but he would be reading the same one for months. Why? I knew he was intelligent but why couldn't he read?

He still couldn't recognise his own name!

When he was nearly seven, he still could not recognise his own name. Each time he changed classes after the summer holidays, he couldn't even find his name on the coat peg in the lobby.

I knew that something had to be done, but I didn't know what to do. Every few weeks, I would go and see his teacher and tell them how worried I was. But repeatedly, and by several different teachers, I was told that 'boys are slower than girls' and 'he will catch up'. With niggling at the back of my mind, I knew that this was wrong!

What should I do?

'... these children are desperately unhappy as they go through their school life being at the bottom of the class, knowing the answers but never being able to put them on paper.'

Like many parents, I felt if I kept saying something was wrong and something needed to be done, it would cause a lot of bad feeling and they might take it out on my child. I didn't know what to do or who to turn to.

Friends said go to the headmistress – but I had spoken to her so many times since Jeremy had been at school and it was not getting any better. Perhaps he really was slow or backward! Perhaps he would never catch up!

It was at that time that a very good friend (and a teacher at this same school) said to me, 'What does it matter if he doesn't amount to anything? You will love him just as much, no matter what he does. At the end of the day, education isn't everything.'

Of course I would love him no matter what he did but that wasn't the point. I believe a mother's love is unconditional. A mother's duty is to protect and provide the best she can for her child. As long as a child does his best then it is irrelevant if her child fails – because he only fails in the eyes of others. But if a child is bright and fails to achieve his potential, then you are failing him if you don't do anything about it.

Was I just an overanxious mother who expected far too much of him? But then what parent wouldn't be anxious with a child who couldn't read at nearly seven years of age? No matter how many times I tried to talk to the teaching staff, no one would listen. We were due to move to another part of the country in a few months and I wanted to try and sort the problem out before the move. How was I going to go about it?

Coming home from school with Jeremy one day, I could tell something was worrying him. As we walked along the road he started to get very upset, saying 'he wasn't the same as the other children, he couldn't read new books or do his maths work'. Finally, distraught with worry, I decided I was going to do something about it.

What was I to do now?

I knew who the educational psychologist was for our area and I contacted him. After explaining the position, he agreed to go into the school that week to carry out some tests. I was too frightened to tell the headmistress! The psychologist confirmed my fears. My son was very bright – but performing well below his ability. He was dyslexic. The psychologist said a plan of action was needed immediately to stop him falling further behind.

Later I was summoned to see the headmistress who was furious at being upstaged in this manner and accused me of going behind her back. I tried to explain that I had been asking for their help for three years and was getting nowhere. She refused to listen and stated that I had made a big mistake and that my son would always be labelled as backward. I knew my son was not backward but there was little point in discussing the matter any further, so I left the office feeling very guilty and worried that I may indeed have caused Jeremy a problem.

'No matter how many times I tried to talk to the teaching staff, no one would listen.'

As soon as I spoke to the psychologist, however, he assured me that I had done the right thing. He explained that some schools were reluctant to call in the professionals and it was best to get the problems sorted out before they got worse. I have since been told by several children that finding out they were dyslexic was fantastic, because before the diagnosis they had always thought they were thick.

It was many years later that I realised that I had infuriated the headmistress through my own naivety, because there is a procedure that parents should follow and that does not involve keeping the Head in the dark!

While waiting for the written report from the educational psychologist to come through, we moved out of the area. My son had only been at his new school for a few weeks and the headmaster had already noticed there was a problem and was prepared to do something about it! The relief was overwhelming.

When the report came, it clearly showed that our son had specific learning difficulties (SpLDs). What on earth did that mean? How could I help? Who else could help and where could I find them? What was the school obliged to do and were they going to do it? The report had raised as many questions as it had answered.

Incidentally, up to that point, my county's psychologist service refused to put dyslexia on their reports. This has now been changed, although I understand there are still a few counties that are reluctant to do so.

Seeking help

'The psychologist confirmed my fears. My son was very bright – but performing well below his ability. He was dyslexic.'

My first point of call was the library and the staff there were extremely helpful. If ever you are desperate to know where to start looking for help, find a good librarian, especially one that's worked in the area for several years. They are worth their weight in gold!

They suggested contacting the British Dyslexia Association as SpLDs often come under the 'dyslexia' heading. The local association explained there were various ways of having your child assessed, one was an educational psychologist's report. The other was an assessment carried out by specialist teachers aimed at identifying areas of weakness and strengths. Once a report was available, an Individual Education Plan (IEP) could be put in place for the school to work around.

Jeremy was offered a place locally with the Dyslexia Association and started attending weekly classes for an hour, and the improvement was quite dramatic. Within a very short period of time, his confidence started to increase because he could see all the other children had the same problems. He realised he was not alone. I knew that the people working in this group were all dedicated to the children and, in almost every case, had first hand experience. Many, many times during the last 25 years, I have had cause repeatedly to thank Deirdre Holland of the Swindon Dyslexia Association and the librarians who gave me the help and pointed me in the right direction. (You can usually find a local branch of the British Dyslexia Association in your area, who will be more than pleased to help you.)

What on earth is a statement?

It was about this time that the school started to talk to us about our other son Mark, who was also falling behind at school. The school explained that they wanted to put a statement on him. Here we go again! What on earth was a statement? It sounds like some official document that you get in the courts or something, doesn't it?

The statementing process simply means putting a Statement of Educational Needs in place. In other words, formally identifying a problem to inform the school and other professional services of the child's needs (see chapter 11).

I worked very closely with the school and other professionals and Mark's Statement of Educational Needs came through very quickly. Some parents call our helpline (at the Swindon Dyslexia Centre) and say that in some cases it takes years to get a statement. This is against government guidance and is usually because the formal procedures are not put into place. Some people leave matters to go on far too long before they formally ask for tests to be carried out.

Is there light at the end of the tunnel?

Yes, yes and yes again. Over the years, both my children have made fantastic progress and are now average/above average in most educational areas. Since leaving university Jeremy has progressed his career from a first line helpdesk analyst to a Senior IT Manager. He has achieved this through hard work and determination and has tried to overcome his dyslexia wherever possible. Mark qualified as a cabinet maker and works for one of the most prestigious firms in the country. So if you feel down about your child, there is light at the end of the tunnel – don't give up!

'... the headmaster had already noticed there was a problem and was prepared to do something about it! The relief was overwhelming.'

The local Dyslexia Association was keen to get me involved with the dyslexia movement, and after a lot of help and advice I opened an organisation called the Swindon Dyslexia Centre for people suffering with dyslexia, dyscalculia and dysgraphia/specific learning difficulties (SpLDs). After nearly 20 years working in the centre, we had to close, due to my rapidly declining health (I have a severe back problem and have had four back operations). The Centre was merged with our other online business, DyslexiaA2Z.com. This website has been operating alongside the Dyslexia Centre for twelve years.

Since our helpline was set up a few years ago, we have helped thousands of people from all over the country and in some cases further afield: America, Africa, Australia, New Zealand and so forth. The parents who telephone say they feel so isolated, that they don't know where to go or who to turn to. We can give independent advice on dyslexia/SpLDs.

'Having received many thousands of calls over the last decade, I realised that there is plenty of help and information available, but the problem was finding it.'

Most of these parents are desperate and at their wits' end to know what to do about their child. If there is not a helpline in your area, how about setting one up? Many parents have the same worries as you do – so you can all support each other (see chapter 22).

Some schools tell parents that their child would have to move to a special school if their child received a Statement for Education. This conflicts with what the Department of Education says. In the vast majority of cases children stay at the same school.

Having received many thousands of calls over the last decade, I realised that there is plenty of help and information available but the problem is finding it.

The Department for Education (DFE) has many excellent leaflets on special educational needs (SEN), but many parents say, 'what is the DFE?' As this information is available free to all parents, why is it not available in the foyer of every school?

Questions, questions, questions?

- Where can I get help?
- What help is available?
- How do you start looking for information?

- What is dyslexia, dyscalculia and dysgraphia?

- What is dyspraxia?

- What is attention deficit hyperactivity disorder (ADHD)?

- What is a Statement of Educational Needs? Should my child have one?

- If he has a statement, will he have to go to a special school?

- What is my child legally entitled to?

- What is the LEA (Local Education Authority)?

- What is the DFE (Department for Education) and where can I find them?

And on and on . . .

These are the sorts of questions parents frequently ask. Although the government has an Education Advisory Service, parents do not know where it is. They produce many different booklets about special educational needs (SEN) but parents are left in awe of the vast array of books. Indeed, in many instances, you have to be widely educated yourself to make head or tail of the information. You also need to know where to get this information from in the first place.

It was at this point that I realised it would be helpful to all concerned if the information was available in one book. This book aims to explain briefly what help is available and where parents can turn to for help and guidance. It is not an in-depth medical book on the types of disorders, but a guide to a few of the hidden handicaps that afflict us.

Summing Up

If you think there is something wrong with your child, then there probably is. Don't be put off with excuses that boys are slower than girls, they'll soon catch up or that the school does not have sufficient money to offer extra help. Be assertive not aggressive, and ask for reading and spelling tests to be carried out. If the teacher says your child's reading level is 2, ask him what the 'reading age' is so that you can understand it better. Depending on the results of these tests you may have to ask the school for a full assessment or an educational psychologist's report.

CHAPTER TWO

Special Educational Needs - Square Pegs Into Round Holes!

Special educational needs covers a wide range of problems from simple hearing or visual difficulties, through the broad spectrum of handicaps both physical and physiological, to some of the severest handicaps of mental handicap. Highly gifted children also come under this category. Many parents of these children feel that they are often denied the help so desperately needed for their education.

There are hundreds and thousands of children struggling to come to terms with their education. Square pegs into round holes; it is very difficult for them to fit into the normal education field.

A lot of people suffer with learning difficulties, many of which are never recognised properly. Many of the disruptive children in schools are naughty simply because they do not fit into the system of sitting, watching and listening that prevails in the majority of education establishments.

These children need more help than the average child, bringing in the problem of extra cost. The average child is allocated 'x' number of pounds for their education, but the children who do not fit into this equation cost the government many, many times more.

Will the schools identify a problem?

The biggest problem seems to be identifying exactly what a special educational need (SEN) is. One school will identify the problems early and start to put in the necessary help. Others will use delaying tactics for years, knowing that eventually the problems will have to be dealt with by another school, college, etc., when the child moves on. Some Local Education Authorities (LEAs) are very good at recognising a child who has problems in the first year or two at school, others are not so good.

Some teachers still believe that if children are born into families where there are lots of books and where adults and other children enjoy reading, children will automatically learn to read. It is their belief that the child slowly builds up the necessary connections between what we say and the marks on a piece of paper. However, for one reason or another, some children cannot seem to pick up these skills automatically and need extra help.

'Parents of gifted children feel that they are often denied the monies desperately needed for their education.'

In this book, I have explained in some detail a few of the hidden handicaps that are difficult to see and therefore difficult to assess. Attention deficit hyperactivity disorder (ADHD) is probably the most notable as teachers and other parents often see it as children who are just spoilt because they are often so naughty.

Summing Up

Special educational needs covers a wide range of difficulties. The biggest problem is identifying exactly what the problem is. Without this it is difficult to put in the correct and necessary help to support the child.

Most children stay in mainstream schooling with some additional help, hardly any go to special schools.

'Some teachers still believe that if children are born into families where there are lots of books, and where adults and other children enjoy reading, children will automatically learn to read.'

Chapter Three

Dyslexia – Specific Learning Difficulties (SpLDs)

Dyslexia (pronounced dis-lex-ia) and specific learning difficulties (SpLDs) often come under the same umbrella which can cause confusion, especially among parents. It is now generally accepted that dyslexia is only one of a group of difficulties that may include: dyscalculia, dysgraphia, dyspraxia and attention deficit disorder (ADD) and attention deficit hyperactivity disorder (ADHD).

The cause of dyslexia is still unknown, pick up any book, type in any search engine and you will find that nobody seems to know entirely what it is. See what two important sites say below:

*The Dyslexia Research Trust states:

> *'The cause or causes of developmental dyslexia are not fully understood, and are the major focus of our research. It is an inherited condition, which appears to affect more boys than girls.'

* Dyslexia Research Trust – www.dyslexic.org. Sept 2011

**The NHS website states:

> 'There are a number of different theories about the causes of dyslexia which all tend to agree that it is a genetic condition that changes how the brain deals with information, and that it is passed through families'.

** National Health Service (NHS) – www.nhs.uk.

'Dyslexia was identified over a century ago, yet little was found out about the causes of dyslexia until about 40 years ago.'

What we do know is that Dyslexia affects approximately 10% of the population; 4% severely. Problems can show themselves in reading, writing, number work, short-term memory, hand control and visual processing. Timekeeping, sense of direction and interpersonal skills can also be affected.

These difficulties often result in great frustration, bearing in mind that dyslexics are usually of average intelligence (many are above average).

How many types of dyslexia are there?

There appears to be three main types of dyslexia:

Acquired Dyslexia

- Trauma, head injury etc. (usually permanent).
- Stroke etc. (temporary or permanent).
- Glue ear. (temporary).

Deep Dyslexia (Primary Dyslexia)

- Family History.
- Linked to chromosomes 6 and 15.
- Damage to left-hand side of brain (cerebral cortex).
- 75-80% male.
- High percentage of left-handedness.

Developmental Dyslexia

- Premature birth.
- Problems with foetus.
- Malnutrition in the womb.
- Poor nutrition.
- Abuse or neglect.

Many of these children are extremely bright in lots of ways, always talking and asking questions, and yet they do not seem to reach their full potential in the academic field. A very good definition of dyslexia is by Dr J E Cullis who wrote: 'Dyslexia means having difficulty with words in reading, spelling and writing – in spite of having normal intelligence and ability.'

Male v Female

There is an ongoing debate as to whether dyslexia affects more males than females. There is some research carried out by Dr Michael Rutter* and his colleagues at King's College London, published in the Journal of the American Medical Association (JAMA), where Rutter suggested that boys are twice as likely to have dyslexia when compared to girls. He based his conclusions on data involving over 10,000 children between ages seven to 15, who had been given standard reading tests in New Zealand and Great Britain. (*Rutter, 2004, 2007-2012). As a result, Rutter insists that his results are strong because 'the studies did not rely on children who were already known to have learning difficulties – a weakness that plagued some previous research'.

In nearly 20 years at the Swindon Dyslexia Centre, we tested thousands of students and would conclude that an approximate 75% to 80% were males. Furthermore, a colleague of mine, who assesses people with visual problems, also supports the 75-80 % male figures as well. So, whilst some people in the dyslexia field still believe in the 50/50 case, we need more research to be carried out to establish the exact percentage.

Dyslexia was identified over a century ago, yet little was found out about the causes of dyslexia until about 40 years ago.

One of the earlier assumptions was that dyslexia was a middle class disease. This came about because people from the 'middle income' bracket could afford to have their children tested for dyslexia, which left people from disadvantaged backgrounds being labelled as slow or backward.

Thankfully, these assumptions no longer exist due to a plethora of research being carried out into the causes of dyslexia. It is now accepted in medical circles that the dyslexic brain is different. It is now indisputable that dyslexia is a neurological condition whose symptoms are most often demonstrated with difficulties in reading, writing, spelling and sometimes numeracy.

'Dyslexia means having difficulty with words in reading, spelling and writing – in spite of having normal intelligence and ability'.

Dr J E Cullis, 1992.

I believe one of the major advances in dyslexia will be made in the area of genetics and it may not be too long before babies are tested at birth, thereby enabling help to be given at a very early age.

Dyslexia is a registered disability under the Chronically Sick & Disabled Persons Act 1970, Education Act 1993, the Disability Discrimination Act 1995 and the Equality Act 2010 (see chapter 20).

Early identification has got to be the key, because once you identify that a child has a learning difficulty and rule out any medical problems, you can start working towards a solution.

Dyslexia in children

Early identification checklist

The signs below may indicate that a pre-school child is dyslexic – they do not need to have all of these problems. However, if these problems continue beyond the time that the average child has grown out of them, they may indicate dyslexia and advice should be sought.

Weaknesses

- Is there a family history of learning difficulties?
- Does the child have delayed or unclear speech, or a lisp?
- Does he have problems getting dressed, putting shoes on the correct feet, doing up buttons, laces, etc?
- Does he enjoy hearing stories but shows no interest in the written word?
- Do people continually say he is lazy and not paying attention?
- Does he have problems with games: skipping, hopping or playing with a ball?
- Does he bump into things and trip over a lot?
- Can he clap a rhythm back?

- Does he often accidentally say that blue is green, red is yellow, etc.?
- Does he often have to search for words and often mislabel them?
- Does he confuse under/over and up/down?
- Can he select the odd word out from lists, for example: cat, mat, pig, fat?
- Can he put things in sequence: numbers up to 10, days of the week and the alphabet?
- Using coloured beads, can he thread green, red, blue and white correctly?
- Does he grip pencils and pens too tightly?

Strengths

- Is he quick thinking and does he have a lot of original thought?
- Is he good at creating things and art?
- Does he have an aptitude for construction games: LEGO, blocks, remote control, keyboards?
- Does he appear bright but unable to do simple things?

Children's checklist

The following signs may indicate a child is dyslexic – they do not need to have all of these problems. However, if these problems continue beyond the time that the average child has grown out of them, they may indicate dyslexia and advice should be sought.

Reading and spelling

- When your child reads and spells, does he frequently:
- Confuse letters that look similar: d-b, u-n, m-n?
- Confuse letters that sound the same: v, f, th?
- Reverse words: was-saw, now-won?

- Transpose words: left-felt?

- Read a word correctly but then read it wrong further down the page?

- Change the words around: the cat sat on the mat (the mat sat on the cat)?

- Confuse small words: of, for, from?

- Have difficulty in keeping the correct place on a line and frequently loses his place?

- Read correctly but does not understand what he is reading?

Writing

Even after frequent instruction does he still:

- Not know whether to use his right or left hand?

- Leave out capital letters or use them in the wrong places?

- Forget to dot the 'i's and cross 't's?

- Form letters and numbers badly?

- Slope his writing even when using margins and guide lines?

- Use punctuation and paragraphs in the wrong places, or not at all?

Other indications

- Is there a family history of dyslexia or similar difficulties?

- Was he a late developer?

- Is he easily distracted or have poor concentration?

- Does he get confused between: left/right, east/west, up/down, over/under?

- Does he have sequencing difficulties: alphabet, nursery rhymes, months of the year, numbers in tables?

- Does he hold a pen too tightly and awkwardly?

- Does he have problems telling the time?

- Does he have problems with tying shoe laces, etc.?

Need2Know

- Does he have short-term memory problems relating to printed words and instructions?

- Does he have mixed laterality (i.e. uses either right or left hands/eyes in writing and other tasks)?

- Does he have particular difficulty copying from a blackboard?

- Does he show confusion with mathematical symbols (plus/minus, etc.)?

- Does he have an inability to follow more than one instruction at a time?

- Is he unable to use a dictionary or telephone directory?

Dyslexia in adults

Dyslexic people are often highly creative and original. They usually succeed through sheer hard work and determination; they are valuable members of a working team.

Many dyslexics excel in areas such as:

- Architecture.
- Arts.
- Computer sciences.
- Construction.
- Electronics.
- Engineering.
- Entertainment.
- Mathematics.
- Physics.
- Sport.

Why people with dyslexia are successful in business

A high proportion of self-made millionaires are dyslexic, probably because they had the tenacity and self-belief to succeed (study by the Tulip Financial Group 2003).

* What makes Sir Richard Branson and Bill Gates successful businessmen? According to Professor Julie Logan, it could be the link she's found between entrepreneurship (people who start their own business up) and dyslexia. Logan's research shows entrepreneurs in the UK are twice as likely to be dyslexic as the general person in the population and three times as likely in the US. Indeed, 10% of UK entrepreneurs are dyslexic compared to just 1% of corporate managers.

*Cass Business School, Feb 2011

It could be that failures in our education system are causing the UK to produce less dyslexic entrepreneurs. This is because the UK system is not identifying the children when they are young. If children were identified at a younger age, then we would probably be producing more people like Branson, Gates etc.

Identifying adults with dyslexia

Many adults who have dyslexia have never been diagnosed as being dyslexic. It is only now that some of them are coming to realise that they have a problem and are seeking help.

Dyslexics often have major problems in a work environment, filling in forms, etc. because they try to hide the problem. Many adults suffer from low self-esteem, lack of confidence and fall short of their employment ability; they are often relieved to know their lack of progress is due to dyslexia and, once diagnosed, they can receive the right kind of help.

Dyslexia and the Equality Act 2010

Dyslexia comes under the Equality Act 2010, which has incorporated most of the Disability Act (see chapter 20). Many employers still fail to get the best from their staff, simply because they do not know how to assist them with their individual problems. The British Dyslexia Association has an essential information pack for employers: 'Dyslexia – An Employer's Code of Practice'. This offers information and advice about dyslexia and how to make 'reasonable adjustments' in the workplace. For further information, go to the British Dyslexia Association's website.

Adult's checklist

Some of the problems listed below may indicate you have dyslexia, but you do not need to have all of them. Do you:

- Have a family history of dyslexia?
- Remember having problems when you were at school?

When reading do you:

- Take a long time?
- Have to re-read the same piece several times?
- Keep losing your place?
- Miss endings off words?
- Do you miss words out?
- Read correctly but not understand what you are reading?

When writing do you:

- Find it difficult to take notes?
- Produce 'messy work'?
- Not know 'where to start'?
- Have poor punctuation?

When spelling do you:

'Many adults who have dyslexia have never been diagnosed as being dyslexic. It is only now that some of them are coming to realise that they have a recognised problem and are seeking help.'

- Make lots of mistakes?
- Have good days and bad days?
- Miss endings off words?
- Reverse letters or leave them out?

Generally, do you have problems:

- Filling in forms, timesheets, etc.?
- Using a dictionary or telephone directory?
- Recalling the months of the year, forwards and backwards?
- Reading maps and directions?
- With left/right?
- With telling the time?
- With time management, getting to appointments on time, etc.?

With numbers do you:

- Have difficulties with mental arithmetic?
- Reverse numbers or leave them out?
- Have problems repeating numbers backwards i.e., 863, 368?
- Mix up numbers i.e., 13 and 31?
- Often dial the wrong telephone numbers?
- Have problems doing sums in your head?

*Famous People with the Gift of Dyslexia

Following are the names of some of the many talented and accomplished individuals who are dyslexic, or had traits associated with dyslexia or related learning styles:

Actors & Entertainers

Harry Anderson

Harry Belafonte

Tom Cruise

Whoopi Goldberg

Jay Leno

Keanu Reeves

Oliver Reed

Tom Smothers

Henry Winkler

Orlando Bloom

Charley Boorman

Danny Glover

Susan Hampshire

Christopher Lowell

Kiera Knightley

Billy Bob Thornton

Vince Vaughn

Loretta Young

Athletes

Rex Ryan, coach

Jackie Stewart, race car driver

Magic Johnson

Greg Louganis

Nolan Ryan, baseball pitcher

Bob May, golfer

Duncan Goodhew, Olympic swimmer

Bruce Jenner, Olympic decathlon gold medalist

Steve Redgrave, Olympic gold medalist (rowing)

Diamond Dallas Page, World wrestling champion

Muhammad Ali, World Heavyweight Champion Boxer

Entrepreneurs & Business Leaders

Richard Branson, Founder of Virgin Enterprises

John T Chambers, CEO of Cisco Systems

William Hewlett, Co-Founder, Hewlett-Packard

Ingvar Kamprad, founder of IKEA

Sir Peter Leitch, New Zealand businessman

Craig McCaw, Telecommunications Visionary

O.D. McKee, founder of McKee Foods

David Neeleman, CEO of jetBlue Airways

Paul J. Orfalea, founder of Kinko's

Charles Schwab, Investor

Ted Turner, President, Turner Broadcasting Systems

Robert Woodruff, President of Coca-Cola, 1923-1954

Frank W. Woolworth

Henry Ford

Artists, Designers, & Architects

Leonardo da Vinci

Ansel Adams, photographer

David Bailey, photographer

Chuck Close

Ignacio Gomez, muralist

Tommy Hilfiger, clothing designer

Pablo Picasso

Robert Rauschenberg

Auguste Rodin

Bennett Strahan

Robert Toth

Andy Warhol

Willard Wigan, micro sculptor

Ian Marley, contemporary artist, South Africa

Jørn Utzon (architect, designed Sydney Opera house)

Filmmakers

Robert Benton

Walt Disney

Nicole Betancourt, Emmy-winning filmmaker

Søren KraghJacobsen (Danish film director)

Inventors & Scientists

Ann Bancroft, Arctic explorer

Alexander Graham Bell

John Britten, inventor

Pierre Curie, physicist (1903 Nobel Prize)

Thomas Edison

Albert Einstein

Michael Faraday

Carol Greider, molecular biologist (awarded 2009 Nobel Prize in Medicine)

Jack Horner, Palaeontologist

Dr. Peter Lovatt, psychologist and dancer

Dr. James Lovelock

Paul MacCready 'Engineer of the Century'

Archer Martin, chemist (1952 Nobel Laureate)

Matthew H. Schneps, astrophysicist

John R. Skoyles, brain researcher

Law & Justice

David Boies, attorney

Erin Brockovich, investigator

Jeffrey H. Gallet, judge

Military Heroes

Thomas Jonathan 'Stonewall' Jackson

George Patton

Musicians & Vocalists

Cher

Brad Little

John Lennon

Nigel Kennedy, violinist

Bob Weir, Grateful Dead guitarist

Physicians & Surgeons

Harvey Cushing, surgeon

Fred Epstein, neurosurgeon

Political Leaders

Winston Churchill

King Carl XVI Gustaf of Sweden

Michael Heseltine

Andrew Jackson

Thomas Jefferson

John F. Kennedy

Gavin Newsom, mayor of San Francisco

Nelson Rockefeller

Paul Wellstone, U.S. senator

Woodrow Wilson

George Washington

Writers & Journalists

Scott Adams, cartoonist (Dilbert)

Hans Christian Andersen

Avi

Jeanne Betancourt, (author of *My Name is Brain Brian*)

Stephen Cannell, television writer and novelist

John Corrigan, novelist

Larry Chambers

John Edmund Delezen, author of *Eye of the Tiger* and *Red Plateau*

Andrew Dornenburg, award-winning author and chef

Agatha Christie

Fannie Flagg (Author of *Fried Green Tomatoes at the Whistle Stop Cafe*)

F. Scott Fitzgerald

Gustave Flaubert

Terry Goodkind fantasy writer, author of *The Sword of Truth* series

Byron Pitts, CBS news correspondent

Patricia Polacco, Children's author and illustrator

Eileen Simpson (author of *Reversals*)

Natasha Solomons, contemporary novelist

Elizabeth Daniels Squire (author of mystery novels)

Bernie Taylor, author of *Biological Time*

Victor Villaseñor

W.B. Yeats

*Famous People with the Gift of Dyslexia. 21 July 2011

Retrieved from Davis Dyslexia Association International, Dyslexia The Gift Web site: http:///www.dyslexia.com/famous.htm.

Summing Up

Special educational needs covers a wide range of difficulties. The biggest problem is identifying a need. Without this it is difficult to put in the necessary help to support the child, student or adult.

Most children should be able to stay in mainstream school with some additional help.

Dyslexia does not stop you getting on in life. Look at the list below of just a few of the many successful dyslexic people.

'Special educational needs covers a wide range of disabilities. The biggest problem is identifying a need. Without this it is difficult to put in the necessary help to support the child.'

Chapter Four

Dyslexia – Testing and Multi-Sensory Teaching

If your child is giving some cause for concern, either because he is not performing at the same level as his peers or appears to be brighter than his peers but is not reaching his potential, then you can arrange for a dyslexia assessment.

Years ago, tests were only carried out after a child had reached seven years of age, or in many cases, even later. These days there are a variety of tests available from five and a half years of age and some even earlier. Some of these tests do not require a child to read or write.

Tests vary from 20 minutes to four hours. The shorter test has value as it can quickly and easily establish whether there is a problem and usually what is causing it. The most comprehensive of all is the educational psychologist's assessment.

All these tests give a good indication of the child's strengths as well as his weaknesses. They also show where the child is at the moment and what he is capable of performing. It is no good expecting a child to be top of the class if he is not able to reach that level, nor is it right that we should accept a child under performing if he is capable of doing better.

There are many different tests and assessments available today and I could not attempt to write about them all. I have listed the ones that I have used and that are well known in the field of dyslexia. The tests and assessments can range from £30 to £500.

Screening

Name of Assessment/Test	Age Range
Aston Index Assessment	5-14 years
Lucid Rapid Dyslexia Screening	4-15 years
Lucid CoPS – Cognitive Profiling System	4-8 years
Lucid Ability – Verbal and Non-Verbal Reasoning	4-16 years
LASS – Lucid Assessment System for Schools	8-11 years
LASS – Lucid Assessment System for Schools	11-15 years
Lucid Exact – Computerised Assessment of Literacy	11-24 years
LADS – Lucid Adult Dyslexia Screening	Adult
LADS Plus – Lucid Adult Dyslexia Screening (Plus Version)	15+ years
Lucid – Memory Booster – Memory Training for Children	Children
Comprehension Booster – Improve reading and listening comprehension 7-14 years	
Lucid – ViSS – Visual Stress Screener	7-adult
Dyslexia Early Screening Test (DEST - 2)	4:6-6:5 years
Dyslexia Screening Test Junior (DST-J)	6:6-16:5 years
Dyslexia Adult Screening Test (DAST)	16:5 years+
Dyscalculia Screener	6-14+ years
Educational Psychologist Report	Any age
Phonological Assessment Battery (PhAB)	6:00-14:11
Phonological Pipa	3:00-6:11
Phonological PAT	5:00-7:00

'Tests give a good indication of the child's strengths as well as his weaknesses. They also show where the child is at the moment and what he is capable of performing.'

The 'Lucid' Screening Systems are available from Lucid and are fully computerised.

The 'Dyscalculia' Screener is available from GL-Assessment.

*Full list of names and addresses at back of book.

A full description of these tests can be found on my website: www.dyslexiaa2z.com

An educational psychologist's assessment is the most comprehensive of all the tests available and also checks the student's intelligent quotient (IQ). Educational psychologists are available free through many schools, colleges and universities. However, they will only be consulted if the school feels there is a long-term problem, and this may take a considerable time to arrange. You can see an educational psychologist privately in order to get your child's needs established quickly.

In the past, students had to have educational psychologists' reports carried out every year in order to receive grants. Recently these rules have changed, if you have one post 16 then you may not need to have another one. More information is available on the Department for Education's (DFE) website. Although a student may not be required to have additional reports, it is often in their own interest to do so. These reports are valuable, not only in assessing progress made but, what is often more important at this stage, identifying the student's need at the current time.

Can I get help to pay for an educational psychologist?

Before you start paying out for any tests, it would be useful to try an online assessment which is usually free. If it shows you have a problem, then that would be the time to have a full educational psychologist's test or similar.

Some private insurance companies fund assessments by chartered psychologists. The referral has to be made via the doctor. It is advisable to speak to your insurance company before making an appointment.

Online dyslexia assessment/tests

Short dyslexia screening assessments can be found online at a few organisations.

Three good sites are:

- www.bdadyslexia.org print out form then work out score.
- www.testdyslexia.com – Ron Davis' Reading Research Council.
- www.beingdyslexic.co.uk – A checklist test to help identify if you may be dyslexic.

Online Dyscalculia Assessment/Tests

Short dyscalculia screening assessments can be found online at a few organisations.

Three good sites are:

- The Dyscalculia Centre, www.dyscalculia.me.uk
- Quizilla, www.quizilla.teennick.com. Go to Quizilla and type in 'dyscalculia' in the search box. Great little website.
- Learning Link Technologies – www.learning-aids.com. Go to dyscalculia section, print out form and mark yourself.

These can be very useful in initially identifying a problem.

Online learning style assessment

Everyone has a preferred learning style. Knowing and understanding our learning styles helps us to learn more effectively. One assessment I found online was from Learning Pride, www.ldpride.net. It gives a very useful tool to help you find out which way of learning is best for you. Another good site is Accelerated Learning, www.accelerated-learning.com. Both of these are very useful when planning an individual learning plan. For instance, it could show something like this: tactile 41%, visual 32% and auditory 27%. The student or teacher can then plan a programme with the main emphasis on using tactile methods.

Multi-sensory teaching

Research has shown that using a structured multi-sensory approach is the best way for students with learning difficulties to successfully overcome their problems.

Multi-sensory means using different senses i.e. hearing (auditory), sight (visual), touch (kinaesthetic) etc. Using an integrated multi-sensory approach, combined with memory, perceptual training and regular over-learning activities, ensures that the student achieves success and is able to participate fully in all areas of the national curriculum.

As the problems are overcome, the student retains the additional abilities that are often developed to help cope with dyslexic problems. These can include highly developed memory for events, sounds and faces, unusual creative skills and exceptional ability in lateral thinking.

Well-established, successful teaching schemes such as Alpha to Omega, Hickey, Units of Sound, 'Nessy' etc., as well as a wide range of educational games and computer-based learning programmes, are used.

A full list of teaching schemes can be found on my website: www.dyslexiaa2z. com/dyslexia and look for 'Multi-sensory teaching packages'.

Studying using different aids

When children start school, particularly secondary school, one major concern for parents of dyslexic children is the amount of homework the child is given – especially with the amount of course textbooks. However, these days, textbooks are not just available as the name suggests in the traditional 'book' style. 'Textbooks' that support the national curriculum from Key Stage 2 to A levels are available in many different formats: cassettes (being phased out); audiobooks which are usually available in MP3 format either on CDs or memory sticks; and films on videos (being phased out) and DVDs .

When books are available in these different formats, i.e., audio and film, it makes it easier for the student to comprehend and remember the information because they do not have to decode the written text.

Audiobooks

There are two charities that supply textbooks on different formats : 'Listening Books' and 'Calibre'.

Listening Books – have thousands of audiobooks for leisure and learning. They support the national curriculum from Key Stage 2 to A level and have many study guides that are not available elsewhere. Anyone can join, membership is currently £20. Choose audiobooks on three easily accessible forms: through the post on CD, downloaded online and 'streamed' from their website.

Calibre – Have thousands of books for coursework and examinations. Membership is free and autiobooks are in MP3 format – either on CDs or memory sticks.

Videos and DVDS

As students start to work towards their GCSEs and A levels, this is the time when it becomes all the more difficult for the dyslexic student. However, in the last few years, more and more work has been transferred to video and DVD. Shakespeare's *Romeo and Juliet*, *Macbeth* and *Othello* are all available on DVD, which is helping students with dyslexia tremendously. One student said after studying the text, it was only when she saw the DVD that it all became clear.

Summing Up

As you can see, there are a wide range of assessments and tests available for identifying dyslexia. Whichever one you choose, please remember that it is imperative to do so early. After identifying a special educational need, it is vital that teachers try to sort out the problems by using a multi-sensory teaching method.

Many parents say that they knew there was something wrong at a very early age, often when the child started playgroup or nursery.

Chapter Five

Dyscalculia

Dyscalculia (pronounced: 'dis-cal-qu-lee-ah') is a specific learning difficulty in mathematics. It was first studied by a Czech psychologist named Ladislav Kosc.

Like dyslexia, dyscalculia can be caused by a visual perceptual deficit. Dyscalculia refers specifically to the inability to perform operations in maths or arithmetic. It could be described as an extreme difficulty with numbers. Dyscalculia does not have the same stigma surrounding it, but it is very important to recognise it as soon as possible before it impacts on a child's self-esteem. Just as there is no single set of signs that characterise all dyslexics, there is no one cause of dyscalculia.

Students may have difficulties with the simplest of numerical tasks, calculations and learning number facts (e.g. multiplication tables). They confuse larger numbers with smaller ones and have problems with simple counting. They often start answering a question and then divide instead of adding or multiply instead of taking away – literally forgetting what they are being asked to do. These factors are often exacerbated by poor processing and sequencing skills and short-term memory problems. They are usually good at answering verbally but cannot tell you how they got the answer.

Dyscalculia is officially acknowledged in England as a specific learning difficulty. (DfES, 2001). We still do not know very much about this condition, however it is estimated 5%* of the population may have it. According to the British Dyslexia Association (BDA), they believe around 60% of people with dyslexia have difficulties with dyscalculia. A lot of research is now taking place and it is hoped that over the next few years we will begin to understand this a little more.

(*Nfer-Nelson May 2002 Dyscalculia: Key Facts for Parents).

The DfES defined dyscalculia in terms of:

'Dyscalculia does not have the same stigma surrounding it as dyslexia, but it is very important to recognise it as soon as possible, before it impacts on a child's self esteem.'

'A condition that affects the ability to acquire arithmetical skills. Learners may have difficulty understanding simple number concepts, lack an intuitive grasp of numbers and have problems learning number facts and procedures. Even if they produce a correct answer or use a correct method, they may do so mechanically and without confidence'. DfES, Guidance to support pupils with dyslexia and dyscalculia, 2001.

Developing a student's skills with sequencing, space organisation, deduction, directional awareness, timekeeping and strategy are essential. The earlier it's started, the better.

Along with dyslexia, the extent to which you can be affected varies tremendously in each individual.

Dyscalculia checklist

Does your child frequently:

- Confuse numbers i.e., 51 for 15?
- Transpose and reverse numbers when reading or writing?
- Confuse minus, subtract and take away?
- Confuse add, plus and add on?

Does he have problems when:

- Learning the times tables?
- Working out simple money and change?
- Estimating numbers: tens, hundreds, thousands?
- Working out percentages?
- Working out averages?
- Understanding fractions?
- Has difficulty understanding concepts of place value, carrying and borrowing?
- Understanding 2+5=7 and 5+2=7?
- Working out the speed in miles per hour?

- Telling the time and concepts related to time such as days, weeks, quarters etc.?

- Learning the date?

- Limited Strategic planning i.e., cannot play games like chess?

- Describing how he got the answer to a mathematical problem?

Summing Up

Dyscalculia may not have the same stigma surrounding it, yet it is very important that it is recognised as soon as possible. If these problems are not picked up at an early age, they impact on a child's self-esteem and can take a long time to correct.

Chapter Six

Dysgraphia

Dysgraphia (pronounced: 'dis-graf-ia') is the inability to write properly, despite a student being given adequate time and attention.

The cause of this disorder is still unknown but it's thought it could be due to a language disorder and/or damage to the motor system. There is ongoing research to try to establish exactly what causes it and how people can be helped.

If people are suffering with dysgraphia, the main sign is that their handwriting will barely be legible. The writing will appear incorrect or distorted and have letters of different sizes and spaces. This could be a ploy because if someone cannot read your writing, they cannot tell if it is spelt properly! Some people with dyslexic-type problems may deliberately write scruffily so people cannot tell if it is spelt wrong. However, it is usually a problem with the actual physical side of writing.

There appears to be several sub-types of dysgraphia:

Dysgraphia Sub-types*

Deuel (1994) divided dysgraphia into three sub-types:

While dysgraphia may be broadly classified as follows, there are many individual variations that affect both treatment and prognosis:

1. Dyslexic Dysgraphia

In 'Dyslexic Dysgraphia', spontaneously written text is illegible, especially when the text is complex. Oral spelling is poor, but drawing and copying of written text are relatively normal. Finger-tapping speed (a measure of fine motor speed) is normal.

'...if someone cannot read your writing, they cannot tell if it is spelt properly! Some people with dyslexic type problems may deliberately write scruffily so people cannot tell if it is spelt wrong.'

2. Motor Dysgraphia

In 'Motor Dysgraphia', both spontaneously written and copied text may be illegible, oral spelling is normal, and drawing is usually problematic. Finger-tapping speed is abnormal.

3. Spatial Dysgraphia

In 'Spatial Dysgraphia', people display illegible writing, whether spontaneously produced or copied. Oral spelling is normal. Finger-tapping speed is normal, but drawing is very problematic.

* Deuel, D. Developmental Dysgraphia 1995.

Will exercise help?

'At the end of the day, what is being tested? The quality of one's writing or the contents of the essay?'

Some people may benefit from exercises to improve fine motor control but for others, despite practising, the problems persist. Handwriting can be improved by regular practice and there are several very good books that may help: *Handwriting Without Tears*, *Why Johnny Can't Write* and *The Handwriting Rescue Kit* available from REM. Occupational therapy may also help.

Developing skills through play

Multi-sensory methods used when playing are the best way to learn.

Playing with things like:

- Practising letter formation in sand/salt trays. (I use cat litter trays – they are very cheap.)
- Using chalk or coloured pens to do letter formation on black/white board.
- Shape and pattern copying.
- Tracing.
- Using Spirograph to practise writing – write, shake it and it goes away.
- Colouring by number.

- Following the line to find out which rabbit belongs to which hutch.
- Threading coloured beads.
- Juggling.
- Swimming.

Some items have been found to be useful, including:

- Pencil grips – help to hold the pencil correctly.
- Templates – help to keep paper in the right place/angle.
- Pre-formed letter shapes – children follow with their fingers.
- Word prediction and speech synthesis software packages.
- Sloping Board Posture Pack (available from Back in Action).
- Dexball (uses 'a unique method to hold a pen' – Insight Medical Products).

Computer versus handwriting

The majority of students with dysgraphia may be able to perform better once they can use a computer. It means that they can concentrate on the actual content of their work rather than what it looks like and the sheer 'mechanics' of writing. I would not normally advocate very young children using computers instead of writing but I think there are always exceptions to the rule and it may be that the student would benefit from this.

However (before I am inundated with letters from teachers, all over the country), I still think children should practise handwriting every day. There are still occasions when we do not have a computer with us and there has been some research which supports the view that when we physically write things down, we remember the 'picture' of the spelling better. (How many times have you tried to spell something aloud and then written it down to check? When you do this it is the 'picture' of the word you are checking.)

Can software help?

There are various software packages to help with dysgraphia such as:

- Word prediction.
- Speech synthesis.
- Spelling programmes.
- Essay and report writing programmes.
- Mind maps and more.

These software packages can help if the only thing stopping a student getting the work down on paper is a physical problem. These programs do take a little getting used to but they save a lot of time, effort and frustration! (See chapter 13.)

Where can I get help with writing?

There are several groups that specialise in handwriting. One is the National Handwriting Association (NHA), formerly the Handwriting Interest Group or HIG. Their main concern is to promote the improvement of handwriting standards in schools and support children with handwriting difficulties.

Another excellent group is the Society for Italic Handwriting (SIC) which launched The Good Handwriting Initiative in 1997. The Society's aim is to promote good handwriting and good teaching. A particular concern is to help teachers at Key Stage 1 (KS1) who wish to begin teaching cursive writing from the first day in Reception.

Practice makes perfect – not always!

I took years and years trying to develop neat handwriting – to no avail! The teachers used to say that 'it looked as if a spider had crawled out of my inkwell and all over the paper'. On one occasion I had to rewrite an essay six times because the teacher could not read it. In the end my mother refused to let me rewrite it again.

At 14 I 'adopted' typewriting as my second form of writing (in those days that was very young). I realised that people could actually read what I was trying to write. In the mid 70s we did not have computers in school so I could not use it for my coursework at the time. (Nearly all schools allow computers to be used now.) At the end of the day, what is being tested? The quality of one's writing or the contents of the essay?

Until we know more about this very complex area, it is difficult to decide what is the most useful way to help the student with dysgraphia.

Signs of dysgraphia

Checklist

The signs below may indicate that someone has dysgraphia – they do not need to have all of these problems. However, if these problems continue beyond the time that the average person has grown out of them, they may indicate dysgraphia and advice should be sought.

- Written text is very poor considering language development.
- Poor motor control.
- Writing is almost impossible to read.
- Mixture of printing and cursive writing on the same line.
- Writing in all directions, i.e. right slant then left slant.
- Big and small spaces between words.
- Different sized letters on the same line.
- Mixes up capital letters and lower case letters on the same line.
- Abnormal and irregular formation of letters.
- Very slow writing.
- Very slow copying from board.
- Does not follow margins.

- Grips the pen too tightly and with a 'fist grip'.
- Holds pen very low down so fingers almost touch the paper.
- Watches hand intently while writing.
- Poor spelling.
- Bizarre spelling.
- Problems with spelling wrong words e.g. 'brot' for brought and 'stayshun' for station.
- Problems with spelling words, e.g. drink as 'brink'.

Summing Up

The problem of dysgraphia may have only recently been recognised but it is very important that we do not just leave it. It took over 100 years for people to start taking dyslexia seriously.

Maybe we should begin to make exceptions for the minority of people who find writing neatly almost impossible to do.

'The problem of dysgraphia may have only recently been recognised but it is very important that we do not just leave it. Dyslexia itself took over 100 years before people started to take it seriously.'

Chapter Seven

Dyspraxia

Developmental coordination disorder (DCD) is a developmental disorder affecting motor coordination. In the UK these difficulties are usually referred to as dyspraxia. You may also hear the term 'perceptuo-motor dysfunction', 'motor learning difficulties' and 'clumsy child syndrome'.

It is not certain what causes dyspraxia but it is thought to be due to an immaturity in neurone development in the central nervous system.

Dyspraxia affects approximately 5-10% of the population, about 2% severely. The overwhelming majority of sufferers are male.

Like dyslexia and dyscalculia, the extent to which people are affected varies tremendously. Recent research suggests that 52% of children with dyslexia have features of dyspraxia (Kaplan 1998). Some people may be affected only slightly, others more seriously. Sometimes developmental milestones are delayed and there could be speech difficulties. This, not surprisingly, leads on to difficulties at school. Often this problem is accompanied by difficulties in vision and movement, i.e. problems with catching a ball.

The Medical Journal defines dyspraxia as:

'A serious impairment in the development of motor or movement coordination that can't be explained solely in terms of mental retardation or any other specific inherited or acquired neurological disorder'.

What a mouthful! I understand it to be:

'If they persistently continue to fall over and are clumsy well after the age their other friends stopped doing it'.

'Dyspraxia affects approximately 10% of the population, some severely. The overwhelming majority are male.'

If you are concerned, you should talk to your doctor, health visitor or special needs coordinator at school (SENCO). You may be referred for an assessment to a number of specialists including a paediatrician, educational psychologist, physiotherapist, occupational therapist or speech therapist.

While there is yet no known treatment for dyspraxia, regular physiotherapy and/or occupational therapy may improve motor and coordination skills. Some children have also shown an improvement by taking fatty acid supplements such as Efalex and eye q (see chapter 18) although there is no firm evidence to support this.

Recent evidence shows that difficulties with dyspraxia do not stop in childhood but continue throughout life.

People with dyspraxia may also experience other problems such as dyslexia, dyscalculia, dysgraphia or attention deficit hyperactivity disorder (ADHD). Recent research suggests that 52% of children with dyslexia have features of dyspraxia (Kaplan 1998).

Further information can be obtained from the charity, the Dyspraxia Foundation.

Dyspraxia checklist

Following is a checklist for dyspraxia. However, you must remember that when children start school they may make several of the mistakes listed. It is only if these symptoms persist beyond the time that the average child has grown out of them that they may indicate dyspraxia and advice should be sought. All children who fall over, drop things and generally take longer to do things are not necessarily suffering with dyspraxia.

Infants

Very young children may have delayed milestones, including problems with:

- Sleeping.
- Being fretful and fidgeting.
- Sitting up (keep falling over).
- 'Bum shuffling' rather than crawling.

- Late walking.
- Talking late and having speech problems.
- Messy eating.
- Baby puzzles or building blocks.
- Picking up small items.

Children

As previously and generally:

- Fidgets constantly.
- Never sits still.
- When sitting, swings his legs and fiddles with his hands and anything else around him.
- Knocks things over.
- Spills things.
- Have problems using knives and forks.
- Bumps into objects all the time.
- Stumbles into doors.
- Falls over for no apparent reason.
- Have problems using stairs and steps.
- Have difficulties standing on tiptoe or one leg.
- Have problems dressing and doing up buttons.
- Have trouble doing shoelaces up.
- Have problems telling the time.

When playing, has problems with:

- Fine motor skills.
- Puzzles, construction games, LEGO, etc.

- Using scissors and craft tools.

- Painting and colouring small areas.

- Threading a needle.

- Catching or kicking a ball.

- Hitting a moving ball, i.e. tennis, etc.

- Riding a bike.

- Using roller skates.

- Difficulties with coordination when swimming.

In a more formal setting, i.e. a classroom, teachers may notice the following problems in a child:

- When reading, has difficulty in keeping the correct place on a line and frequently loses his place.

- When writing, grips the pencil very tightly and awkwardly.

- When writing, changes hands constantly and does not know whether to use his right or left hand.

- Writes in different directions on the same paper.

- He does not use margins.

- His writing slopes on page.

- He has difficulty copying symbols, i.e. circles, squares and triangles.

- He has difficulty copying work from whiteboards, etc.

- He has difficulty following instructions.

- He has difficulty reading maps.

Summing Up

While there is still no known treatment for dyspraxia, physiotherapy and occupational therapy may help improve motor and coordination skills. There are lots of things you can do at home to help, for example balancing games, trampettes, wobble boards, standing on one leg, etc. Most importantly, these things are fun.

Chapter Eight

Attention Deficit Hyperactivity Disorder ADHD/ADD

Attention deficit hyperactivity disorder (ADHD) has been known about for a long time. It has undergone several name changes, at one time being known as 'hyperkinesias' (Latin derivative for 'super active'), hyperactivity, attention deficit disorder (ADD) and latterly, ADHD (with or without hyperactivity). As with other problems mentioned in this book, there are different degrees of severity. Many children with ADHD display features of dyslexia and dyspraxia.

A child who can't concentrate, moves around constantly, has poor school performance (in contrast with his intelligence) and has disruptive behaviour may be suffering with ADHD. There is evidence to suggest that children with this problem could eventually be expelled from school and/or worse, be in trouble with the police. Until recently it was assumed that children would grow out of ADHD, however it is now known that over a third of children will continue to have symptoms in adulthood.

At times all children may be overactive and inattentive, but hyperactive children are disruptive nearly all the time. ADHD is thought to affect between 3% and 7% of the school-age population. While there is evidence to suggest that the overwhelming majority of children with ADHD are male, there is some research to suggest that this could be because girls often have the mainly inattentive form of the condition. This may show up as the child being quiet and dreamy and therefore they are not actually being identified as having ADHD.

'There is evidence to suggest that children with this problem could eventually be expelled from school and/ or worse, be in trouble with the police.'

Are there different types of ADHD?

There appears to be three subtypes of ADHD:

1. The predominantly hyperactive impulsive type.

2. The predominantly inattentive type.

3. The combined type (which makes up the majority of cases).

People with ADHD appear to be intensely restless and impulsive: if they think about something, they do it – sometimes with disastrous results! They have a hard time focusing on things and get bored after just a few minutes. They often find it difficult paying attention for the shortest possible time, thereby causing problems with organisation and completing routine tasks.

Diagnosing ADHD

In order to make a diagnosis of ADHD, the symptoms usually:

- Start before the child is seven years of age.
- Cause real problems in at least two areas of the child's life, e.g. school and home, work, etc.
- Are long-term, i.e. last more than six months.

When assessing for ADHD, it is important that everyone concerned with the child is given the chance to participate in the assessment. This comprehensive study should include:

- Family history.
- Behaviour as a baby – restless, noisy, screams, etc.
- Behaviour as a toddler.
- Medical development.
- Behaviour at pre-school.
- Behaviour at school.
- Behaviour at home (which can sometimes be worse or better).

For further information on ADHD check out an excellent book, *ADHD - The Essential Guide* (Need2Know).

Oppositional Defiant Disorder (ODD)

Many children with ADHD have oppositional defiant disorder (ODD). This disorder is defined by negative and disruptive behaviour, especially towards authority figures such as parents and teachers.

Who can help me with my child?

There are various ways and people who can help children with ADHD. These include:

- Psychotherapy.
- Cognitive behaviour therapy (CBT).
- Physiotherapy.
- Teacher training.
- Classroom support.
- Support groups for the children and their parents.

What can I do to help my child?

There are lots of ways of making things easier on your child and yourself. Some ways include:

- Praise, praise and praise.
- Try to ignore bad behaviour (when it is safe to do so).
- Always reward good behaviour.
- Make sure you are directly looking at the child and make eye contact when you speak to him.
- Give one instruction at a time.

Does medication work?

Some people think by giving medication to children suffering with these problems, they will become drug dependent. However, there appears to be little scientific support for this argument. Children who are deemed in need of medication after extensive tests should be given the opportunity of using it.

Medication, where appropriate, should only be used with other forms of treatment, i.e. psychotherapy, behaviour therapy, etc. and should be reassessed regularly. The most common form of medication used is methylphenidate (Ritalin). This type of medication is still seen by some groups as extremely controversial. However, if you are one of the many desperate parents who have tried everything else, they are seen as a necessary evil.

Dextroamphetamine (Dexedrine, Adderall) used to be recommended but has now been withdrawn by the National Institute for Clinical Excellence (NICE).

'The women, who had no scientific or medical qualifications, noted that children with hyperactivity or ADD often had other symptoms such as excessive thirst, dry skin and allergies.'

Where can I get help for my child?

Sally Bundy MBE, is the founder and director of the Hyperactive Children's Support Group (HACSG). The group was founded by Mrs Bundy and her late mother, Mrs Vicky Colquhoun, to help people who found themselves in a similar situation to one they were experiencing some years ago.

It was in 1980 that Mrs Bundy and Mrs Colquhoun put forward a radical proposal to the medical profession, suggesting a link between people with ADHD and a lack of fatty acids in their diet.

They were the first people to take on the medical experts to prove that they knew more than them about the causes of hyperactivity in children.

The women, who had no scientific or medical qualifications, noted that children with hyperactivity or ADD often had other symptoms such as excessive thirst, dry skin and allergies. They carried out a survey of over 200 children with hyperactivity and concluded their problems were linked to biochemical imbalances. These were caused by a deficiency of essential fatty acids (EFAs). Two of these fatty acids are supplied by evening primrose oil and it was noted that there was an improvement in hyperactivity by children who took the oil. The scientific establishment, however, never took it seriously.

After almost 15 years, an American journal of clinical nutrition confirmed Mrs Colquhoun and Mrs Bundy's findings. There has since been extensive research that has also confirmed their earlier findings that some dyslexic children can be helped with EFAs.

There are now several supplements available, two of which are Efalex and eye q, that contain these missing fatty acids. These supplements are available in liquid, tablet and 'chews', which make them much more palatable for children to take.

Mrs Bundy has continued to work tirelessly to raise awareness of ADHD and in 2005 she was awarded an MBE for her work. Further information is available on her group's excellent website, the Hyperactivity Children's Support Group (HACSG). See the help list.

Another useful site is that of ADDISS, the National Attention Deficit Disorder Information and Support Service.

Case study

'My son Miles was born hyperactive and the only treatment offered was an endless succession of drugs, none of which were effective. Being unhappy about the long-term effect of these, I decided to try and find out all I could about this problem. It seems that in some cases hyperactivity is aggravated, if not caused, by intolerance to some chemical additives in food, notably colourings, flavourings and preservatives. Consequently, I eliminated these from his diet, with very encouraging results.'

Sally Bundy, MBE founder and director of Hyperactive Children's Support Group (HACSG).

The Mental Health Foundation has also published a free information booklet on ADHD.

Do artificial colourings in food cause behavioural problems?

After decades of debate concerning artificial food colourings in food and the link with children's bad behaviour, it was gratifying to see that the research carried out below finally appears to support the lobby against food colourings being added to our foods.

* In 1987 the HACSG, with the support of Professor Neil Ward, Senior Lecturer in Chemistry at the University of Surrey and the group's Scientific Director, found that, out of a total of 357 children who had been diagnosed as hyperactive, 87% had adverse reactions to artificial colourings and 72% to artificial preservatives in food.

*Hyperactive Children's Support Group – website home page.

ADHD/ADD checklist

The signs below may indicate that a person has ADHD, but they do not need to have all of these problems. However, if these problems continue beyond the time that their peers have grown out of them, they may indicate ADHD and advice should be sought.

Infants

- Often distressed.
- Extreme restlessness.
- Poor sleep pattern.
- Difficult to feed.
- Excessive and constant thirst.
- Dry skin.
- Frequent tantrums.
- Screaming.
- Head banging.
- Rocking the cot.

Children

- Generally fearless and impulsive.

- Do not stop to think.
- Take undue risks.
- May dash around.
- May run out into roads.
- Erratic behaviour.
- Accident-prone.
- Increased activity – always on the go.
- Compulsive touching of everything and everyone.
- Clumsy.
- Talk incessantly.
- Allergies.
- Sleep and appetite problems continue.
- Poor coordination.
- Difficulty tying laces.
- Difficulty dressing.
- Problems with handwriting.
- Difficulty with ball games.
- Lack self-esteem.
- Problems with making friends.
- Impatience, so they will not take turns in games.
- Demands must be met immediately.
- May hit out and grab things.
- Inflexible personality
- Uncooperative.
- Defiant.
- Disobedient.

In a more formal setting, i.e. the classroom, teachers (as well as seeing the above mentioned behaviour) may notice the following problems in a child:

- Poor concentration and brief attention span.
- Sitting through lessons is almost impossible.
- Fidgets constantly.
- Constantly moving feet, hands, etc.
- Taps pens, pencils, books, etc.
- Roams around classroom.
- Cannot take turns.
- Blurts out answers to questions.
- Speaks entirely inappropriately and out of turn.
- Has a weak short-term memory.
- Normal IQ but under-performs at school.

Adults

Most of the features of ADHD in childhood remain.

- Employment may be difficult because of relationship problems and poor memory.
- Antisocial behaviour may become so extreme it leads to trouble with the law and to excess alcohol consumption.
- Poor self-esteem may be distressing.

Summing Up

There has been a lot said over the years on the subject of ADHD, most of it negative, blaming parents and branding children as just being naughty. It has been over 25 years since a link with fatty acid deficiency was found and it is about time that there was a routine assessment available so all children can be tested for it.

Chapter Nine

Gifted Children

I make no apologies for including the gifted child in this book. Although these children do not come into the special educational needs definition, their educational needs in many cases are still not being met. The fact that these children are gifted should and does mean that the LEAs have a duty to provide extra support for them – over and above their peer group.

There are various degrees of giftedness in the same way as there are varying degrees of learning difficulties. Some children are gifted in a particular area, e.g. maths, art or music, but in this chapter I am concentrating on children who are gifted overall.

In March 2004, David Bell, the government's chief inspector for Education, addressed the National Association for Able Children in Education, saying that gifted pupils should be put on a special educational needs register in the same way as those with learning difficulties. He went on to say that some primary schools in particular were failing to meet the needs of gifted pupils. If gifted students were put on a register, it would be easier to provide them with an Individual Education Plan (IEP) so they could be monitored regularly.

There still does not appear to be a standard way of identifying gifted children in our schools. All LEAs appear to be 'doing their own thing', some better than others.

Dr Peter Congden realised over 30 years ago the desperate need for gifted children to be identified, and set up the Gifted Children's Information Centre. Along with a few other organisations he has been working hard to bring this to the notice of the government's advisors. In 2002, some 30 years after Dr Congdon's work began, the government finally recognised what these agencies had been saying for years and set up the National Academy for Gifted and Talented Youth (NAGTY). This programme was very successful; however it was replaced in 2007 by the Young Gifted and Talented (YG&T) programme. Unfortunately, this academy has also been closed. It is difficult

'There are various degrees of giftedness in the same way as there are varying degrees of learning difficulties.'

getting the needs of gifted children recognised, when so many schools still fail to recognise gifted children. Ofsted's Annual Report 2009-2010, which was published in November 2010, highlights that schools are not challenging these children. Paragraph 75 of the report states:

'For more academically able pupils, inspection evidence shows that teaching and learning can be insufficiently challenging and poorly matched to their needs'.

With Ofsted confirming that schools are not giving the right level of work to gifted children, it is more important than ever, that teachers do their best to help identify these children and give them the encouragement and the correct level of work to stretch enquiring minds and to enable them to reach their full potential.

Intelligent Quotient (IQ) tests

For parents who suspect their child is gifted, it is important to organise an independent psychologist's test. The child will take part in a lot of different tasks, after which you will receive a report listing your child's strengths and weaknesses and, more importantly, it will give you an IQ level for your child. When you have the results, schools can use the report to make an Individual Education Plan (IEP) for your child.

What exactly is giftedness?

There are different levels of giftedness in the same way as there are varying degrees of learning difficulties.

There are many online companies that offer free basic IQ tests. One of the largest run every year in the UK is Test the Nation, run by the BBC. You can find it at www.bbc.co.uk/testthenation. These are very useful to take part in. Depending on the results, you may wish to take a more thorough test. Another couple of companies offering free tests, include: Free-IQ Test.net - available at: http://www.free-iqtest.net or IQ Test.com – available at: http://www.iqtest.com.

Mensa

What does Mensa mean? It is not an acronym. It is Latin for 'table'. It denotes a round table where all members are equal.

Mensa was founded in England in 1946 it is a society for very clever people with a high *IQ. People, from all walks of life, whose IQ is in the top 2% of the population can join Mensa. Mensa has over 105,000 members worldwide. British Mensa has more than 24,000 members in the UK, including 900 junior Mensans (under 18) – one of these is just 2.6 years of age (at 2008).

Anyone can take a supervised intelligence test to see if they are eligible for membership. You can take a test with Mensa or supply evidence of testing by a qualified psychologist.

*Mensa uses many IQ tests, including:

1. On the 'Culture Fair' test (British Mensa), a score of 132, places a candidate in the top 2% of the population.

2. On the 'Cattell B111', a score of 148 or above would be required (and would still be in the top 2% of the population).

All Mensans are in the top 2% by IQ, whichever scale their intelligence was measured by.

Gifted Children's Information Centre

In 1978, Dr Peter Congdon founded the Gifted Children's Information Centre. Its principal function is to publish and disseminate information on the subject of gifted and talented children. Over the years, as demand for publications and books has grown, Dr Congdon has addressed many international conferences on giftedness and left-handedness, written numerous articles and books on gifted and dyslexic children, and is the author of the new *Ant to Zip* series. This is a structured phonic programme for teaching, reading, spelling and handwriting to all children, and especially of use to those with dyslexia/SpLDs.

'Mensa was founded in England in 1946 and has over a 100,000 members from all walks of life, worldwide. It is the society for very bright people.'

Organisations that can help the gifted person

There are several organisations that help and support children, parents, teachers and other professional groups. A few of these include:

- Gifted Children's Information Centre.
- National Association for the Gifted Child.
- The Support Society for Children of High Intelligence (CHI).
- Mensa.
- Pullen Publications (specialises in books for able pupils).

Giftedness checklist

The following signs may indicate whether someone is 'gifted or talented' – they do not need to show all of these signs.

Generally:

- Does not appear to fit in with standard curriculum.
- Has good general knowledge.
- Has a much larger vocabulary than his peer group.
- Has a highly developed verbal aptitude.
- Is interested in many subjects.
- Works well on his own with very limited intervention.
- Will accomplish a variety of things earlier than other children.
- Understands instructions well.
- Concentrates well.
- Is good at problem solving.
- Learns easily and remembers quicker than his peers.

- Will be the best one in his class.
- Will rapidly respond to new ideas.
- Will think of new ways of doing things.
- Is very curious.
- Is very imaginative.
- Generally asks more detailed questions.
- Produces more elaborated answers.
- Is more deeply engaged in testing.
- Is often a group leader.
- Can juggle far more activities and interests than their peer group.
- Has strong opinions.
- Gets on with adults better than his age group.

With mathematics:

- Has a high level of reasoning.
- Understands processes.
- Can complete calculations easily.
- Has a high level of visual spatial ability.

With reading:

- Probably read before he started school.
- Reads a book quickly.
- Has a good ability to decode words.
- Can comprehend complex printed passages.
- Memorises well.

When writing:

- Has highly developed ideas.
- Produces illegible handwriting, (because his brain is working faster than he can write, so ends up scrawling in haste to get it all down).

Appears to be very talented in (some not all):

- Music.
- Art.
- Creative writing.
- Scientific thinking.

Summing Up

We should pay particular thanks to people like Dr Peter Congdon who have worked tirelessly to promote giftedness and dyslexia over the last 25 years. It is most important to get these children recognised as early as possible. By identifying a need, you can start to put in the necessary help to support the child. It may be some time before children are routinely screened for giftedness and their needs put into place, but at least we have now made a start. It may be that with the growth of the Internet, more and more gifted children will be taught at home.

Chapter Ten

How Can I Get Help?

What do I do if my child needs help?

If you are concerned that your child is underachieving at school, you should talk to his teacher. Many parents try to express their concerns with teachers early in the morning, but this can cause problems because mornings are very busy for the teacher who has 30+ children in their classroom. Almost all these children will need some help with coats, buttons, zips, etc. After school is probably best but it can help if you give the teacher a little time to prepare for you.

The fairest way for all concerned would be to explain quickly after school that you are concerned and ask if you could make an appointment in a couple of days' time. Not only can the teacher be prepared for it, but so can you. Parents tell me they still feel extremely intimidated when they go to the school. I felt the same way for many years – it took me more than 10 years to finally feel at ease. Don't let them make you feel that way! You are a grown-up too!

'Parents tell me they still feel extremely intimidated when they go to the school... Don't let them make you feel that way! You are a grown-up too!'

First things first

It is very important that you keep records of all contact with the school. You can do this simply and easily in a cheap little diary. Every time you speak to anyone at the school (even by telephone) about your child, write down what was said. You will see why this is a valuable exercise later. Don't forget, do it now! You will only forget if you put it off.

The first appointment

Make a list so you can go through it when you see the teacher. Why are you concerned?

- Worried about your child's reading?
- Worried about his spelling?
- What progress is he making compared to other pupils in his class?
- Is he receiving any additional help?
- He doesn't seem to have many friends?

And so on.

If you are worried about your child then you probably have cause to be – a mother does know best! After you have discussed everything with the teacher, tell him you will monitor the situation and contact him in about a month to see if there is any change in the situation.

Make a diary entry for one month's time. When the time is up, if there has been no significant improvement and you are still concerned about things, contact the teacher again and make another appointment.

'If you are worried about your child then you probably have cause to be – a mother does know best!'

The second appointment

Once again, make a list before you go. Work down your list together and explain what progress you have found, if any. If the teacher feels that things are improving and he would like more time, tell him you will monitor the situation for another few weeks. Once again, go home and make a reminder in your diary for a month's time.

The third appointment

If after this time you feel there still has not been any significant improvement and you are still concerned, ask for another appointment. Before you go to the next meeting, write a letter with the points of concern. Ensure you make two copies of this letter.

When you see the teacher, listen to his point of view and exchange ideas. Then if you are still not happy, point out that you have waited over three months for things to improve and you are extremely concerned at your child's lack of progress. Explain that due to the lapse of time you would like the matter looked into officially. Address this letter to the Head of the school but give a copy to the teacher and keep a copy in your diary or folder.

Whenever you send a letter to the school or education authority, you should always bear the following in mind:

- Always send your letter in the post.

- Send it Recorded Delivery if you prefer (you pay a little extra for this at the post office and someone at the school has to sign for this, so you know they have received it).

- If you are sending a copy of the letter to anyone else, it is usual to put the letters CC at the bottom of the page and put the name of the person you are copying the letter to. The post office can usually make a copy of the letter for you at a small charge.

- If you are answering a letter from the education authority, always check to see if they have put the initials CC at the end of their letter. If so, you should copy the letter to that person as well.

- When writing, always assume the person you are writing to does not know anything about your child; it makes it easier if later on if you have to contact a solicitor.

- Always, always make a copy for your own file and keep it safe.

The letter could be something like this:

Your Name
Your Address
Your Postcode
Your Telephone No.

1st January 2009

Mr A Smith
Head of the School
Anyschool Secondary Modern
Anytown
Wiltshire
SN22 99

Dear Mr Smith

Re: Peter Jones – D.O.B: 1st May 2000

As you are aware, I have been working with you since (look in the diary) concerning Peter's lack of progress.

I am particularly concerned that he is still not able to read, spell and write properly. Peter is becoming more and more withdrawn. Every evening he gets frustrated when attempting to do his homework and then gets very upset. He is lacking in confidence and now has very low self-esteem.

I think that Peter has dyslexia or a specific learning difficulty, therefore, I wish to refer him for a 'Statutory Assessment' under the 1989 Education Act, (Page 42, Code of Practice), so we can get the correct help for him quickly.

I understand you have a time limit of six weeks to indicate that you will or will not make a 'Statutory Assessment'.

I look forward to hearing from you soon.

Yours sincerely

Mr Christopher & Mrs Maria Jones
CC Class Teacher

You can now see why it is vital to keep a list of the dates of every visit to the school and what the outcome of each meeting was. This is extremely important in officially identifying an educational need. These notes will be needed later on.

Once you have given a letter to the teacher (and a copy to the head teacher), you are effectively asking for the first stage of the assessment procedures to be put into place (see chapter 11).

What happens next?

Reports will be compiled from everyone who has dealings with your child to see exactly what the problems are. After looking at all the paperwork from teachers, the education authority and the doctor, the LEA will make a decision as to what help your child needs, if any.

How long does a statutory assessment take?

The 2001 Education Regulations set out time limits for the testing procedures. The process of making a statutory assessment and a statement should take 26 weeks.

'The Code of Practice gives practical guidance on how to identify and assess children with special educational needs.'

In England and Wales, the organisations Network 81 and the BDA have 'befrienders' who can talk you through the Code of Practice and how to succeed. They may be able to go along to meetings with parents. They also have leaflets on getting help for your child with special educational needs.

A more detailed description of the assessment procedure can be found in chapter 11.

Health, Education and Social Care (HESC)

From 3rd November 2010, the Special Educational Needs and Disability Tribunal (SENDIST) ceased to exist as a standalone body and became part of a new two-tier 'First Tier Tribunal' and the 'Upper Tribunal'. The two new Tribunals consist of chambers that group together jurisdictions dealing with similar work or requiring similar skills.

Health, Education and Social Care (HESC) – First Tier Tribunal

Any parent who cannot reach an agreement with their local Authority (LA) about their child's special educational need, can appeal to the First Tier Tribunal.

Health, Education and Social Care (HESC) – Upper Tribunal

If a parent is not satisfied with the First Tier Tribunal's decision, they can go to the Upper Tribunal, instead of to the High Court.

Further information can be found at Her Majesty's Courts and Tribunals Service. Website: www.justice.gov.

'Allow the teacher time, but if there is no real progress you must begin formal procedures as soon as you can.'

Scotland and Northern Ireland – the Code of Practice

The Code of Practice in Scotland and Northern Ireland differs slightly from the England and Wales.

Scotland

The Scottish Parliament passed new legislation under the Additional Support for Learning (Scotland) Act 2004, changing some of the 1984 Act. See below for details:

- Special Educational Needs was replaced by Additional Support Needs.
- Provision is no longer outlined in the Record of Needs.
- The criteria for Additional Support Needs is no longer confined to children with a disability.
- Coordinated Support Plans were instituted.
- Requests can be made for all children or young people who have Additional Support Needs.
- New Mediation, Dispute Resolution and Tribunal services were implemented.
- The legal rights of parents, children and young people were altered.

Northern Ireland

The Education (Northern Ireland) Order 1996 amended by the Special Educational Needs and Disability (Northern Ireland) Order 2005 applies. It is similar to England and Wales and states that statutory responsibility for securing provision for special educational needs children lies with the Education and Library Boards and Boards of Governors of mainstream schools.

Summing Up

Speak to your child's teacher as soon as you realise there is a problem. Don't get put off over and over again. Obviously allow the teacher time, but if there is no real progress you must begin formal procedures as soon as you can – ensuring the child's needs are identified and any help is put in place as soon as possible.

Don't worry about the assessment procedures – there are lots of people who can help you through this difficult time.

Chapter Eleven

How to Obtain Help for Your Child's Special Educational Needs

By Dr D Cowell B.Sc. M.Phil. Ph.D. Dip. Psych.

The most important law dealing with special educational needs is the 1996 Education Act. This act is explained in the Special Educational Needs Code of Practice. An updated version was published in 2001. The Code of Practice gives practical guidance on how to identify and assess children with special educational needs.

All early education provision, Local Authority Schools and Local Education Authorities must take account of this code when they are dealing with children who have, or might have, special educational needs. Professional reports must take account of the Code of Practice and provide the required detailed information.

Health and social services must also take account of the code when helping Local Education Authorities.

The basic principles of the Code of Practice are as follows:

- All children with special educational needs should have those needs met.
- Most children with special educational needs will have those needs met in ordinary schools.
- The views of parents must be taken into account at all times.

- Children with special educational needs should receive a broad, well-balanced education which, as far as possible, is based upon the national curriculum.

- The wishes of the child should, as far as possible, be taken into account.

The term special educational needs has a legal definition. Children with special educational needs all have learning difficulties or disabilities that make it more difficult for them to learn than most other children of the same age.

The law says that children do not have learning difficulties just because their first language is not English. Of course, some of these children may have learning difficulties as well.

'Approximately 20% of children will have special educational needs of some kind at some time during their education. A few children, approximately 2%, will need substantial extra help for all their time in school.'

Approximately 20% of children will have special educational needs of some kind at some time during their education. A few children, approximately 2%, will need substantial extra help for all their time in school.

Here are some examples of special educational needs. A child has difficulties with:

- All the work undertaken in school.

- Some activities: reading, writing, number work, remembering information.

- Expressing themselves or understanding what others are saying.

- Making friends and getting on well with adults.

- Physical or sensory difficulties.

- Behaving properly in school.

- Organising themselves.

- Some kind of sensory difficulty, for example with hearing or eyesight.

- Some physical difficulty which may affect their learning or adjustment to school.

The Special Educational Needs Code of Practice provides the framework for action. Schools are required to have their own special educational needs policy. They are also required to have a person in charge of special needs. Such a person is normally called the special educational needs coordinator or SENCO. The school is required to follow a graduated approach. This means that they have to set up a step-by-step plan to resolve, or clarify, the exact nature of the child's difficulties.

The school must inform the parents when they start to give extra or different help for the child. In early education, this help is called Early Years Action. In normal schools, this help is called School Action. If the child does not make sufficient progress, the class teacher or the SENCO will then talk to the parents about obtaining advice from other specialists outside the school. They might want to ask for help from, for example, a specialist teacher, an educational psychologist, a speech and language therapist or another help professional. This kind of help is called Early Years Action Plus or, in the case of schools, School Action Plus.

The SENCO will include the parent in discussions and will consider parental views in making decisions. SENCOs should keep parents fully informed about the child's progress.

At the stage of School Action or School Action Plus, the child will normally have an Individual Education Plan (IEP).

The IEP should say:

- What special help is being given.
- How often the child will receive help.
- Who will provide the help.
- What the targets for your child are.
- How and when your child's progress will be checked.
- What help you can give your child at home.

As a parent, you can approach your child's teacher or the SENCO at any time. In some areas there is a Parent Partnership Service that can give the names of local voluntary organisations and parents' groups which might be able to help.

Sometimes the School Action and School Action Plus does not succeed in fully resolving the child's difficulties. Such children, who have long-term and specialist requirements, will be considered for a Statement of Special Educational Needs. This is normally described as a statement. This statement describes all the child's needs and all the special help that he or she requires. Approximately 2% of children will enter special schools or units.

Children who require long-term special help normally have a statutory assessment. This is a detailed investigation to find out exactly what your child's special needs are and what special help the child needs. A statutory assessment is only required if the school or early education setting cannot provide all the help that your child requires.

Your child's school or early education setting can ask the Local Education Authority to carry out a statutory assessment. They will always talk to you before asking the LEA.

Similarly, you can ask the LEA yourself to carry out the statutory assessment. However, you should always talk to your child's teachers or the SENCO before asking the LEA.

If the LEA decides not to assess your child, you can appeal to the First Tribunal to ask them to change the LEA's decision. Alternatively, if the LEA wish to carry out the statutory assessment and you do not agree with this, you can go to the tribunal in the same way.

If the LEA carries out a statutory assessment, they will ask a number of professionals employed in the public sector to give their views on your child. The LEA will ask for advice from:

- The teachers in your child's school or early education setting.

- An educational psychologist.

- A qualified medical practitioner.

- Social services (who will only give advice if they know your child).

- Anyone else whose advice the LEA considers appropriate.

Parents have the right to be present at any interview, medical or other test during the statutory assessment. Sometimes the professionals may ask to see the child without the parents as children sometimes behave differently when parents are present.

Parents should provide a written record of their views as part of the statutory assessment. Parents can also send the LEA any private advice or opinions that they have obtained. The LEA will take these into account as part of the assessment.

As part of the assessment process, the LEA will send parents details of schools which are suitable for children with special educational needs.

Parents have a right to say which Local Authority School they wish their child to attend, either mainstream or special. The LEA must agree with the parents' preference as long as:

- The school you choose is suitable for your child's age, ability and special educational needs.

- Your child's attendance will not hinder the education of other children already at the school.

- Placing your child in the school will represent an efficient use of the LEA's resources.

You may wish your child to go to a school which is not run by an LEA. This could be a non-maintained special school or an independent school that you feel can meet your child's needs. The LEA will consider your wishes carefully before they make a final decision, but if there is a suitable state school, the LEA have no legal duty to spend public money on a place for your child at a non-maintained or independent school.

After the statutory assessment, the LEA may decide to draw up a Statement of Special Educational Needs. If you disagree with what is in the statement, you should first ask the named officer of the LEA for an explanation. If you are still not happy, you have the right to appeal to the First Tribunal with reference to:

- Part 2 – the description of your child's special educational needs.

- Part 3 – the help to be given to your child to meet those needs.

- Part 4 – the type and name of the school which the LEA thinks your child should attend.

The LEA will tell parents about the local arrangements for resolving disagreements. This is normally the appropriate course of action before appealing to the First Tribunal.

The LEA must keep your child's progress under review and ensure that the statement continues to meet their special educational needs. The review of the statement must occur at least once a year but LEAs can review it more often if necessary.

If your child has a Statement of Special Educational Needs, the Annual Review in Year 9 is particularly important in preparing for their move to further education, higher education and adult life. The review will discuss a Transition Plan for your child's move to adult life.

Education for young people with special educational needs does not stop at 16+. Depending on their abilities and requirements, they can stay at an ordinary or special school, or can move to a college of further education or into work-based training. Children who leave school to attend further education will not normally keep the statement. However, the college will continue to monitor their progress and give appropriate help.

The First Tribunal only deals with a limited number of situations, as described above. However, if your complaint is about something else, you may be able to take matters to the local government Ombudsman. An example of this would be if the LEA did not keep within the required time limits.

The Department for Education and Skills (now called Department for Education) produces a guide for parents and carers entitled *Special Educational Needs (SEN)*. In this publication, the important point is made (page 3) that parents may wish to talk to someone who is independent and knows about special educational needs.

The booklet goes on to say that you can get help from the local Parent Partnership Service or from national or local voluntary organisations, which are mainly charities.

One reason for obtaining independent advice is that the person you see may be able to be more objective than somebody who is, for example, employed by the LEA with whom you are negotiating.

Another advantage is that you can seek help from a person of your own choice. For example, you could refer to your own psychologist or medical practitioner. Many private practitioners have long experience in specialised areas of special educational needs. They will usually have substantial experience in either the Health Service or Local Education Authorities, or both.

Private practitioners will normally subscribe to a code of practice laid down by their professional body. They are also likely to have their own professional indemnity insurance.

A further advantage is that the private practitioner would be available to you if the child moves to a new school or if you move to a new area. Within LEA or National Health Service settings, such moves usually involve a complete change of the professional personnel who have been involved with your child.

Families who have private health insurance can sometimes obtain the help of a private practitioner through the insurance scheme. In such cases, the *Special Educational Needs* booklet makes it clear (page 16) that private advice must be taken into account as part of the assessment by the LEA.

Two names and addresses are particularly important for parents to know about. Firstly, the Special Educational Needs Tribunal *(SENDIST) provides a special booklet which can be obtained from the LEA or from the SEN Tribunal. You can find out more about the local government Ombudsman in a special booklet, obtainable from the LEA or from the Ombudsman's office.

*The SENDIST arrangements have been changed with effect from 3rd November 2010.

There is now a two-tier structure, known as the First Tribunal and Upper Tribunal.

Initial appeals by parents against the proposed decisions of Local Education Authorities will go by the First Tribunal. Subsequently, an appeal may be lodged by parents to the Upper Tribunal. (See chapter 10, Section, Health, Education and Social Care (HESC).

These changes are likely to require parents to seek, and pay for, advice from legally-qualified individuals (i.e. solicitors and barristers), rather than educational psychologists.

This is because the appeals process will concern itself more with notions of precedent and definition.

However, educational psychologists will continue to play an important role. This will include carrying-out detailed diagnoses preferably over long periods of time; explaining the difficult issues related to statistical and clinical prediction; being aware of the advantages and limitations of standardised tests; understanding the possibilities of common end unusual teaching and remedial techniques.

There is a perception among psychologists that this type of work can only be carried out effectively by a very experienced practitioner – and one whose specialism is directly relevant to the case going to appeal. For these reasons, suitably-qualified psychologists will be hard to find and the costs will be high.

Educational psychologists employed by the local authority are usually perceived by parents as members of the cohort of paid officials ranged against them. However, at least in theory such psychologists are required by the terms of their professional role, to be impartial, and indeed, many such psychologists are known to have resisted pressure to change or modify their views.

A problem commonly experienced by parents, is the essentially hierarchical nature of the Local Education Authority. For example, the education psychologist who has advised the family, and may indeed have supported them, might not be available to appear before the First Tier or Upper Tribunal. Local Education Authorities could send a Principal or Senior Educational Psychologist or an 'Education Officer', on the grounds that such a person has a wider or more detailed overview of the issues involved.

An important point for parents to bear in mind, is that no longer is the Local Education Authority required to pay for the best possible educational placement for a pupil regardless of cost. Such an obligation was removed about twenty years ago. Tribunals are now required to take account of costs, as well as possible educational outcomes.

A word of caution must be offered to any parent who is considering embarking upon what is likely to be a lengthy, exhausting, and possibly frustrating appeal process.

In most families, time, energy and money are limited. There is a danger that efforts over a period of months or years will adversely affect relationships within their family, brothers and sisters of a child who is the subject of an appeal can feel ignored or resentful at the considerable expenditure of family resources on a single member.

A further word of caution is due with regard to the reasons for the appeal. Personal experience shows that some families have embarked upon a course of action for which there is little evidence. Many courses of 'treatment' or educational procedures are based on remarkably little evidence and cost many thousands of pounds every month, for perhaps years.

Here are three examples of 'lost causes' which the author has been closely associated with over the years.

Over a period of approximately 5 years, a company began offering programmes to cure a range of conditions from dyslexia, through to dyspraxia, to attention deficit disorder (ADD), and attention deficit hyperactivity disorder (ADHD). The programme consisted of a set of exercises which were said to be based upon those performed by 'spacemen', who allegedly suffered dyslexic-type symptoms after spending time in gravity-free conditions.

The second involved the dubious idea that children would make better progress in literacy if they were given 'counselling' this was based on the idea of improving 'self-esteem'.

The third was based upon a nineteenth century theory of 'recapitulation'. The programme involved several hours of exercises every day, which were designed to reactivate the walking and balance reflexes of our reptilian and ape-like ancestors.

In all the previously mentioned examples, and no doubt in many other cases, no scientific evidence was available. Nevertheless, the vendors of these schemes not only managed to obtain worldwide publicity for their claims, but they were able to recruit well-meaning and sincere members of the public to work for them.

Enquiries about the value for the programme were invariably answered by producing inspiring stories of those that made astonishing progress after all other methods had failed. However, in general the only 'evidence' available was that issued by the company selling the programme.

Scotland and Northern Ireland

Scotland and Northern Ireland have a separate Code of Practice. For further details of the Code of Practice, please see chapter 10.

Chapter Twelve

The Role of the Psychiatrist

By Dr R Eyre

Consultant in Child and Adolescent Psychiatry

Introduction

Every district has its own Child and Adolescent Mental Health Services. These may be found within a hospital setting or in a community-based clinic. They also may carry different service titles, e.g. Child Guidance, Child and Family Consultation, Child Psychiatry. In the past, such clinics were often run in partnership with education and social services, but nowadays they tend to be NHS resources. Referrals are accepted from all professionals working with children and often from parents themselves.

'Only in a minority of cases do children have mental illnesses seen in the adult population.'

Only in a minority of cases do children have mental illnesses seen in the adult population. The majority of children will have emotional or behavioural difficulties that they and their families can see are causing them problems in their normal social or educational progress. There will often be stressful factors in the background contributing to the presenting problem. These could include family break-up or relationship problems, bereavements, chronic physical illness and school difficulties. The Child and Adolescent Mental Health Services have a range of professionals who may be able to offer help, including psychiatrists, clinical psychologists, family therapists, community nurses, psychotherapists and specialist teachers. All these people will have regular links with schools and nurseries and the local authority.

'Research shows us that children with specific learning difficulties are more likely to develop later conduct disorders than children without those problems. It is, however, not an inevitable progression. . .'

Special learning difficulties

Dyslexia is certainly one problem that may cause stress and distress in a child, leading to possible emotional and behaviour difficulties if it is not detected and appropriately managed in school. Most child psychiatrists prefer to use the term 'specific learning difficulties' rather than dyslexia.

A child has a specific learning difficulty when his or her performance on a certain learning task (reading, spelling, numerical skills) falls 28 months behind that which would be usual for that child's age and overall ability. It can lead to many difficulties in the classroom setting. Often, such children have good oral verbal abilities, so it can be confusing and upsetting for them not to be able to translate this ability into their reading, writing or spelling skills. It can also be confusing for class teachers who may see a child as underachieving or unmotivated rather than having a specific problem.

It is not difficult to see that children will often feel bad about their difficulty and may seek to avoid it by distracting behaviour away from the educational activity. They may develop a low self-esteem and become anxious about school. They may be seen as misbehaving or disruptive in class when they avoid the work that is difficult. If the problem is not recognised, the child can move on to becoming a child with behavioural difficulties.

Research shows us that children with specific learning difficulties are more likely to develop later conduct disorders than children without those problems. It is, however, not an inevitable progression since it is more the maladaptive responses of the child and others to the learning difficulties that lead to a poor outcome rather than the learning difficulties per se.

Specific learning difficulties may be associated with other problems too. Poor coordination, difficulties with concentration and over activity are more often seen in children with these difficulties than on average.

Management issues in specific learning difficulties

The Child Mental Health Services can be helpful in:

▪ Addressing secondary behaviour difficulties.

▪ Assessing overactivity and poor concentration.

▪ Detecting or diagnosing specific learning difficulties in the above as a presenting problem.

▪ Advising other professionals and agencies.

Psychological testing is always necessary to diagnose specific learning difficulties, and ordinarily an educational psychologist would do this. Sometimes, however, the clinical psychologist with Child and Adolescent Mental Health Services can also contribute to the assessment.

Once the diagnosis has been made, the most important next step is that parents and professionals alike are aware of the specific areas of difficulty that the child has. The Education Department will then make special needs provision for the extra teaching input necessary, and it is helpful for parents to have regular communication set up with their child's teachers. Sometimes extra tuition from specialist teachers outside of school may be helpful, so long as there is good communication between school and tutor.

Acknowledgment of the problem and appropriate educational measures can go a long way towards improving concerns over a child's difficult behaviour or low self-esteem. Sometimes the child and their family need ongoing support and help with these issues, and this is where Child and Adolescent Mental Health Services can continue to help after the diagnosis has been made.

Chapter Thirteen

Computers and Dyslexia/SpLDs

During the last decade there have been tremendous strides in the field of technology. There is such a vast array of specialist software for people with learning difficulties of any type, that I can only provide an overview of the types available.

Can computers help with dyslexic students?

Computers are now an important part of classroom teaching. Although no computer package can ever be a substitute for good teaching, the correct software packages can help and support the busy teacher. Many programs can be incorporated into a specialist-teaching scheme. They provide over learning, structured and systematic teaching, immediate reinforcement and feedback, and the additional motivation that students require to succeed.

The advantage of instant feedback and the possibility of echoing each letter name, each word, each sentence of any marked section of text, as well as reading through, helps the student with poor short-term memory and ensures an efficient transfer to long-term memory – making learning fun. Software packages can provide structured learning, continually developing skills and providing support for literacy and numeracy.

How can computers help learners?

Computers can help people with learning difficulties in lots of different ways:

- Learning to use databases and spreadsheets may aid sequential thinking and problem-solving skills.

- They can motivate people, especially children.

- There is immediate reinforcement.

- Students have the ability to make and self-correct mistakes in private.

- They provide essential over learning/reinforcement.

- Most computers can now be programmed to 'speak to you'. This software could revolutionise foreign language learning. Programs with speech make learning truly multi-sensory.

- Students can listen – ideas developed orally can be tried out and changed   easily.

- Response is immediate.

- Students work at own pace.

- Printouts and text on a screen are often easier to read than the student's own writing.

- Reading and spelling are incorporated into nearly every program.

- The colours and brightness on computer screens can be adjusted.

Computer equipment – hardware

The first three items are the bare minimum when using computers. The remaining items are useful. What hardware the student needs will depend on their individual difficulty.

1. Computer, (preferably laptop, notebook, 'tablet' or other handheld device.

2. Internet and email.

3. Printer with built-in scanner, if possible.

4. Portable USB memory sticks.

5. Electronic gadgets.

Specialist computers or keyboards

6. Keyboard (ideal for people with disabilities).

7. Touch screen computers (ideal for people with disabilities).

8. Hands-free computers (ideal for people with disabilities.)

1. Laptop computers, 'tablet' or other handheld device

Laptops, 'tablets', or other handheld devices are the most popular computers these days because of their size. They can range from just £299. Most computers in this range incorporate speakers and sound cards (i.e. multimedia) that make it ideal for specialist educational software.

2. Internet and email

The Internet is invaluable for research and emails. If you do not have it at home, almost all schools, colleges and libraries allow free access.

3. Printer

There is a vast array of printers on offer. Many printers now incorporate scanners so you do not have to have a separate one.

4. Portable USB memory sticks

A Portable USB Memory Stick CD 8GB costs about £5.00 and is an excellent investment as you can download data and transfer it to other computers. Information can be downloaded quickly onto a small stick (which looks like a pen).

'Although no computer package can ever be a substitute for good teaching, the correct software packages can help and support the busy teacher.'

5. Electronic gadgets

There is a wide range of electronic gadgets available today, specifically for the dyslexic user. You will find a large selection of them from a company called iANSYST.

6. Keyboards – for nursery/Key Stage 1 children or children with dyspraxia)

BigKeys is a starter keyboard and has a lowercase keyboard. It has been designed for nursery/Key Stage 1 children and it has a colourful and uncluttered layout in the traditional 'qwerty' style. All unnecessary keys are removed or hidden. The very large keys are colour coded – vowels are yellow, 'r' is red, 'b' is blue, etc. – further aiding letter recognition. This beginner's keyboard makes an excellent start before changing to the standard keyboard. It is very easy to use; no software needed – just plug in and go. An excellent choice for very young children. Further information from KeyTools.

7. Touch screen computers

These computers look like any other monitor but they work by simply touching the screen with your hands. They are very useful in identifying and assessing children (of three years plus) for early signs of specific learning difficulties.

8. The hands-free computer

Hands-free computers use neither screen, keyboard nor mouse. Hand movements control them in mid-air. The 'virtual computer' is used in some offices and operating theatres. Hand movements in mid-air are picked up by cameras coupled to pattern recognition software and used to control the computer in the same way as a mouse does. These systems cost more than conventional computers. However, their use for people with disabilities is infinite.

Software

There are probably thousands of software packages available now. I have only included a few of the most tried and tested ones which support reading, spelling, numeracy, writing skills and organisational and planning skills.

1. Word processor, spreadsheets and database.

2. Speech recognition software (SRS), sometimes known as voice recognition software (VRS).

3. Word prediction and speech synthesis.

4. Reading and spelling.

5. Punctuation.

6. Grammar.

7. Handwriting.

8. Maths.

9. Mind mapping.

10. Study skills.

11. Speech training.

12. Games.

1. Word processor, spreadsheets and database

A word processor is the most important piece of software required. People with learning difficulties are finding that when they use a word processor, 'the written world opens up' to them. Most good word processors incorporate a spellchecker and a grammar checker.

I prefer to use Microsoft Office XP software – this is very simple to use and has a good spellchecker and grammar checker included. It also has spreadsheets, database and speech recognition built in (see below). Many offices use this software. Most schools allow students to use computers to complete GCSE coursework and some examinations.

2. Speech recognition software (SR or SRs)

During the last few years, speech recognition software has come a very long way. Some of these software packages are now rated independently to be 97% accurate. If you are buying a new computer, make sure it is a certified 'speech recognition ready machine'.

This software works by 'talking' to your computer. As you talk, the words are written on the computer screen – and they are spelt correctly. This type of software helps to improve spelling because the student always sees the correctly spelled words. The computer types up exactly what you say. The golden rule is to speak slowly when recording your own voice, stressing 'a', 'an', 'and', etc., but please do not speak like a robot!

'During the last few years, speech recognition software has come a very long way. Some of these software packages are now rated independently to be 97% accurate.'

Office XP now has voice recognition software built in. However, if a student has dyslexia or dysgraphia, in my opinion they would find it easier to use separate voice recognition software, such as the one below.

Dragon Naturally Speaking 11.5

This easy-to-use speech solution allows you to create, edit and revise documents without using a keyboard. This software is one of my favourites and in my opinion, is one of the best on the market for dyslexic students. Price approximately £85. You can get further information from REM.

3. Word prediction and speech synthesis

Word prediction and speech synthesis software 'predicts' what the student wants to say by 'guessing' what the word is from the first couple of letters. With some of these packages the computer will search the list for the appropriate word, i.e. type the letter 'a' and several of the common words are suggested such as a, an, and, another, etc. The user can normally listen to the words being spoken thus helping them decide which word is correct.

ClaroRead Plus

The ClaroRead Plus is a word prediction program which includes ScreenRuler (a strip-magnifying program), the new ClaroView screen tinting program and Scan2Text which uses the powerful OmniPage optical character recognition for turning paper and PDF files into editable, speaking Word documents. Further information available from REM.

Penfriend XP

This software is able to predict words before they are typed, saving time and effort. It can also speak its suggestions and read text from documents. A great help for those with dyslexia. It has been so successful it has been sold to all schools in Northern Ireland as well as all UK online centres in colleges and libraries (nearly 900 centres). You can get further information from REM.

Penfriend XP - Portable

As above, but is portable. It's ideal to take from classroom to classroom or office to home. You can get further information from REM.

Read and Write Gold (10)

Providing the ultimate support for dyslexic students and adults, this toolbar offers a variety of tools. Combinations of speech-feedback, phonetic spellchecker and dictionary and word predictions help overcome the problems of accessing and composing written material. It can correct words such as 'there', 'they're', and 'their' where the sound of the word is correct but the context may be wrong. This product was shortlisted for the prestigious Education Resource Award 2010 in the category of Best Special Education Resource. You can get further information from iANSYST.

4. Reading and spelling

Wordshark 4 (5-15)

This is one of the best reading and spelling software packages. Based on Alpha to Omega by Dr Beve Hornsby and Frula Shear, it is used in hundreds of establishments across the country. There are hundreds of word lists with lots of games to help reading and spelling. The lists include the National Literacy Strategy high-frequency words and you can also add your own word lists. Designed for Key Stages 1-2 word lists and KS3 subject word lists, but is also great for secondary and adult users as it includes higher level word lists. Available from iANSYST.

Units of sound Version 5 (9-adult)

This multi-sensory reading intervention program also develops spelling skills. The structured, cumulative program builds reading accuracy, vocabulary, sentence writing, spelling comprehension and listening skills. It includes a screening test to ensure placement at the correct level. Suitable for Key Stage 2 to adult. Available from Dyslexia Action.

Nessy Learning Programme (5-adult)

Nessy is a structured learning programme that uses games and fun to teach. It covers all the reading, spelling and writing skills you need, going from the alphabet right through to an adult standard. Available from iANSYST.

GAMZ Player CD (7-adult)

This is based on the popular GAMZ card games. It has many additional features and activities to support reading, phonics and spelling. Available from iANSYST.

5. Punctuation

The Punctuation Show

An excellent package for teaching the rules of punctuation. Many activities explain and then go over basic skills. Areas covered include apostrophes, brackets, hyphens, dashes, capital letters, full stops, commas, semicolons, colons, speech marks, question marks and exclamation marks. Available from www.dyslexic.com.

Penfriend XP

This software includes a smart punctuation function, which enables 'penfriend' to correct user's punctuation as they type. A great help for those with dyslexia. You can get further information from REM.

Read and Write Gold (10)

See Read and Write Gold (10), under 'Word prediction and speech synthesis'.

6. Grammar

The Grammar Show (7-14)

This helps children learn and consolidate their understanding of grammar. Suitable for Key Stages 2 and 3. Areas covered: nouns, simple verbs and tenses, verb forms, adjectives and adverbs, pronouns and prepositions, sentences and standard English. Available from www.dyslexic.com.

7. Handwriting

Handwriting Without Tears (7-14)

Millions of students all over the world use this program. An easy-to-teach, easy-to-learn curriculum makes handwriting mastery joyful for students and their teachers. I can really recommend this product. Comes with paper, already lined and is easy to explain to the student.

Nelson Handwriting Series (Reception to KS2)

This is a 'whole class' teaching tool that supports the Nelson Handwriting series. Goes from Reception to KS2. Animation with voice-overs for all the letters and joins will provide teachers with a motivating tool for teaching core skills. Pupils can participate on the whiteboard copying and tracing letters and patterns. The discs include printable worksheets for each letter or join for individual practice in the classroom or home.

8. Maths

Numbershark (5-16)

One of the best maths packages but needs some adult supervision for programming. The structured learning task covers the four main rules of number, addition, subtraction, multiplication and division. Available from REM.

Key Stage Maths Invaders (all ages)

An excellent package to practise basic number skills by playing 'space invaders'. Available from Amazon.

MathMania

Key Stage 2 (7-11 years)

Develop maths skills, by practising and developing the 'four rules' of number.

Angles, Time, Measurement, Shape & Space.

Key Stage 3 (11-14 years)

A variety of exciting maze-worlds, children practice and develop their maths skills by answering questions on numbers, time, etc.

9. Mind mapping

Some dyslexics prefer a visual working environment. Mind mapping software makes it easy to get ideas down and then rearrange them into order. They can be used to brainstorm, write essays, revise projects, take notes, etc.

Inspiration v9 (7-adult)

An excellent visual learning tool. A great computer program that maps out ideas in a nifty spider chart. Helps students develop ideas while planning and structuring workflow. Available from iANSYST.

10. Study skills

Technology has made studying so much easier for all students – not just dyslexic ones. Many programs can help with time management, planning, note taking, reading and writing.

WordsWork

This programme is written primarily for dyslexic adults. It uses a multi-sensory approach for helping the older dyslexic student improve their study skills. WordsWork has very good graphics and uses humour to encourage students to develop a variety of language skills. Using a 'learning style' approach, students are encouraged to identify and use their strengths to overcome areas of weakness. Available from iANSYST.

11. Speech training

Computers are now helping children at some schools to learn to speak properly. A speech training aid computer displays the word it wants a child to say and listens to the way the child repeats the word. It then tells them if they have said it correctly. Once the child has said the word correctly, he can move on to the next word.

There are thousands of words with graphics available. Teachers using the software are impressed at the computer's ability to 'hear' them talking. The Defence Research Agency and Hereford and Worcester County Council initially developed the project jointly.

12. Games

I am including games in this section because many parents often see arcade type games as children 'just playing'. But playing these games can help develop hand/eye coordination, and a fun approach is adopted to make learning almost painless. Sinking battleships in alphabetical order is far more exciting than looking for X, Y, Z, etc. on a keyboard!

Accessories

1. Portable dictionaries and spellcheckers.

2. Recording equipment.

3. PDAs – personal digital assistants.

4. Quicktionary Reading Pen II.

5. Portable word processors.

1. Portable dictionaries and spell checkers

Franklin UK English dictionary/thesaurus (11-adult)

This pocket sized Collins UK dictionary, thesaurus and phonetic spellchecker weighs less than 100g. It contains a comprehensive dictionary and thesaurus. Features include LCD screen, word games and ROM card slot. It is the ideal portable solution for dyslexic students. Available from iANSYST.

PageMark electronic dictionary

This is absolutely superb; it is called PageMark because that is exactly how thin it is. You can slide it into any book you are reading, and it is always at hand to help you.

It includes over 145,000 words, phrases and definitions from the Compact Oxford English Dictionary and automatic spelling correction.

Franklin Literacy Word Bank (5-11)

Designed to support the National Curriculum and National Literacy Scheme. Includes a portable dictionary, thesaurus and spellchecker. Perfect for young children in Key Stages 1 and 2. Available from iANSYST.

2. Recording equipment

Digital voice recorder (11-adult)

Several of these are available, including the Olympus VN-1200 Digital Voice Recorder. An easy-to-use, small device, with a powerful memory. This is an excellent recorder for note taking and dictation and can be linked directly to the computer.

Micro cassette recorder (7-adult)

Lots of these are now on the market; they are very small and compact, and are excellent for taking notes in the classroom. The Sony M800V is an excellent choice, ultra slim with good sound quality and extremely small compared to a normal tape recorder.

3. PDAs (personal digital assistants)

PDAs give you one big advantage over any other small computer – you can view and edit data while away from your main computer. They are very useful for people with dyslexia and short-term memory difficulties. Most of them have the ability to set reminders for appointments, create 'to do' lists and read and edit documents. There are two main operating systems: Windows Pocket PC2000 and the Palm operating systems. Both allow you to synchronise your documents with Windows applications on your home computer.

Palm Tungsten C (PDA) (14-adult)

View and edit MS Office documents on the move and keep track of appointments and tasks using the software provided. Available from iANSYST.

Palm Zire 71 (11-adult)

Get organised with the Palm. Synchronise appointments and contacts with your PC ideas and notes on screen. Available from iANSYST.

4. Quicktionary Reading Pen 11, Oxford edition (11-adult)

This portable reading pen has been designed specifically for people with dyslexia. It literally 'reads' words aloud and is just a little bigger than a normal pen. Glide the pen over a word, see it on the display and then hear it read and spelt out loud – it will even give pronunciations. It has been used successfully in schools, colleges, libraries and resource centres.

5. Portable word processors

AlphaSmart Neo 2 (5-adult)

A popular, inexpensive battery-powered word processor with easy, one-key transfer to PC for formatting. This high-powered keyboard is a must for writers and students at all levels, can hold over 4,000 pages of single spaced text. KAZ Typing Tutor included. Very long battery life. Available from REM.

Agents for software

Here are just a few of the companies that sell software:

- REM.
- iANSYST.
- Dyslexia Computer Resource Centre.
- AVP.
- Dyslexia Educational Resources.
- SEN Marketing.

Computers in examinations

Special arrangements

The Examination Board Regulations for Special Arrangements state that these arrangements are made to enable candidates with a disability (e.g. dyslexia/ SpLDs) to show their attainment when otherwise they might not be able to do so. (Special arrangements should not give an advantage over other candidates.)

Each examination board is different. The school has to check in advance with the relevant board to ascertain exactly what the student can use. This must be done in good time.

Any special arrangements must have been recommended by an educational psychologist and the report must state the exact nature of the special arrangement required. However, in order to free up time with educational psychologists, some specialist teachers, who have additional training, can now arrange for a reader, extra time, etc.

Some special arrangements can include:

- Use of a word processor (spellcheckers to be turned off).
- Use of typewriter.

'A lot of dyslexic people say when they use a computer, "the written world opens up to them".'

- Use of speech recognition software in examinations.
- Extra time.

The British Dyslexic Computer Committee

The British Dyslexic Computer Committee has been reviewing programs for dyslexia for many years. There are a series of booklets which are updated frequently. For further information, contact the BDA.

Summing Up

Computers are a great help in education. Over the last few years, in relative terms, they have become cheaper, making them more accessible for the average family. Specialist software has also greatly improved and become a lot cheaper. You can get software to help you learn a language, play the piano or even learn to cook.

A lot of dyslexic people say when they use a computer, 'the written world opens up to them'.

Chapter Fourteen

Selecting a School and Private Tuition

It is very difficult for anyone to offer advice on the type of school you should be looking for, as every child's needs are so different. The majority of children will simply go to the school in their immediate vicinity, but specialist schooling is slightly different because there is not usually a lot of choice. It is best to speak to as many people as you can, including teachers, the Education Authority's advisors and other parents – the decision is then up to you.

It is important that the correct school is identified for your child. Sometimes, although a school is on your doorstep, it may not always be the best one for your child's special needs. Visit all the schools in your area and see what specialist provision they can offer.

There are many different types of schools. These are just a few:

- Mainstream schools (your local school).
- The independent sector.
- Dyslexia schools.
- Schools for deaf children.
- Schools for blind children.

State schools – mainstream

The majority of schools in the country are operated by the government/LEAs. Most of these are ordinary mainstream schools.

Even if children have special needs, i.e. dyslexia, dyspraxia, etc. the child usually stays in mainstream schooling. This is usually considered best for the child and the family. It is only in extreme cases (if the school cannot meet the needs of the individual child) that they would go to a specialist school. Some mainstream schools have units attached to them for dyslexia, etc. or therapists and other specialists can come into the school on a regular basis.

A booklet is available from your LEA with a list of all schools in your area.

Independent schools

There are two main bodies that deal with the independent sector: CReSTeD and the Independent Schools Council (ISC).

CReSTeD

This is the Council for the Registration of Schools Teaching Dyslexic Pupils, and it maintains a list of schools that meet CReSTeD criteria. You can obtain a copy of all schools free from CReSTeD.

The Independent Schools Council

The Independent Schools Council has a comprehensive list of the majority of schools in the independent sector. It has details of all schools on its register and in what the school specialises in (if anything).

The ISC represent approximately 1,300 independent (or private) schools in the UK. These schools charge parents to send their children to them. Some LEAs pay to send pupils to private schools, although, as you would expect it is difficult to get them to agree to this. There is sometimes help available towards the school fees. Some private schools are boarding and others are day schools.

Grants

It is very difficult to obtain a grant for dyslexia as there are always so many applicants chasing a very small pot. However, there are several organisations which may be able to help and reference books are usually available in the library. One book that deals solely with grants is *Guide to Educational Grants 2011/2012.,* by Sarah Johnston., published by DSC, £75. You should be able to see a copy of this book in your local library.

Schools for Dyslexics

The majority of schools that specialise in dyslexia are private (at the moment, I think there are just a couple in the state sector). Some of these schools are just for dyslexic pupils; the others have dyslexic units attached to them.

These schools are usually the best place for children with severe dyslexia. Children who attend these schools enjoy themselves because they are 'the same' as everyone else. The majority of these schools take students for a period of time (approximately two years) and then the children go back into mainstream schooling.

There are specialist schools for SpLDs/dyslexia which are approved by the Independent Schools Joint Council and the Council for the Registration of Schools.

The Portage Service

The Portage Service (National Portage Association) is a home-visiting educational service for pre-school children with additional support needs and their families. It aims to support the development of young children's play, communication and relationships and to encourage full participation in day-to-day life within the family and beyond the home. Ask your health visitor for more information or look at the Portage website: www.portage.org.uk.

Pupil referral units (PRU)

Pupil referral units (PRUs) provide education to children who, because of illness, exclusion or other reason, do not/cannot attend mainstream schooling. Children usually attend a PRU for a fixed period of time and then return to mainstream school.

Schools for the blind and deaf

Many charities including the RNIB and the RNID have several specialist schools. They also give help, guidance and training to mainstream schools so the majority of children can stay in their local schools.

Other schools

This covers a very wide area of specialist schools including art, science, drama, behaviour, handicapped, dyspraxic and many others.

Education centres

If your child is struggling at school then private tuition can make all the difference. There are quite a few private education centres around the country that operate between 9.00am to 5.00pm, Monday to Friday and Saturday mornings. These centres have thousands of pounds for specialist teaching and testing equipment. Children usually work for one-hour sessions.

The school can make an 'approved absence' for an education activity. The children usually come out of school for an hour once or twice each week. Most schools are quite happy for this – the children may miss a little time at school but it means they are not tired at the end of the day and so can progress rapidly. I personally do not think we should expect children to do extra work after school each day (on top of their usual homework). My own children would certainly have kicked up about it!

The fees for these centres are usually approximately £30-£50 per hour.

Private tutors

There are many private tutors who work from home in the evening. They usually charge approximately £15-£35 per hour. Lessons take place after school. Word of mouth is the best recommendation but please make sure the teachers:

- Are suitably qualified with a SpLD qualification.
- Regularly update their knowledge with suitable courses.
- Have references available and that you see them.
- Have certificates confirming police checks (from the Criminal Records Bureau or CRB) and that you ask to see them.

When teaching, does the teacher:

- Use a multi-sensory program such as Hickey, Alpha to Omega, Nessy, Games Player, etc.?
- Feel qualified to undertake further assessments as necessary?
- Have computer software to reinforce what the child has learnt and to stop the child from being bored?
- Follow the recommendations from any psychologist's/school report?
- Liaise with the school as necessary?
- Give homework each week?
- Assess/test at regular intervals?
- Give out regular progress reports, and do they charge extra for them?

Checklist for selecting a school

Selecting a school for your child is not always easy. The school nearest to you may not be the best one to help your child.

Below is an example of what your checklist for selecting a school should include.

General

- Ask the school for a prospectus.
- Visit the school on a normal working day.
- Find out if the school has a home/school contract.
- What does the school do about discipline issues?
- All schools have to have an anti-bullying policy, ask to see a copy.
- Try to meet all teachers who will come into contact with your child, especially the special needs staff.

Specialist teaching unit – staff

- How many specialist staff are employed at the school?
- What qualifications do they have?
- Does the school provide in-house training for SpLD teachers?
- Do teachers keep up to date with special needs courses?
- How many times do other professionals such as psychologists and speech therapists (if applicable to your case) come into the school?
- Do dyslexic children have to take foreign languages? (Some schools allow children to withdraw from these lessons, so the student can have more special needs help.)

Specialist teaching unit – students

If your child has specialist tuition:

- How many hours is it for each week?
- How is it arranged?
- Are the lessons carried out individually or in a group? How many are in a group?

'It is best to speak to as many people as you can, including teachers, the education authority's advisors and other parents – the decision is then up to you.'

- When are these lessons held? (It is important that it is not during your child's favourite subject.)

- Who takes these lessons and what are their qualifications? (Sometimes schools use 'helpers' with no experience at all.)

- How often do they monitor progress?

- When do they call in the appropriate specialist help, i.e. psychologist, etc.?

- How are details of the child's learning difficulties passed on to other non-specialist staff?

- Are you kept up to date with the progress or concerns?

Specialist equipment – general

- Does the school use special equipment, e.g. computers, tape recorders, voice recognition software (VRS), etc.?

- Does the school use specialist software (recommended by the BDA)?

- Will students with special needs be able to use laptops, computers, notebooks, tablets, palm-held organisers, PDAs, etc., for their coursework?

Dyslexia-friendly schools pack

The Dyslexia-friendly schools pack is an excellent resource pack, (it is frequently updated) and is free to download, and available to primary and secondary schools. It has information, tips and ideas on how to make school dyslexia-friendly.

The pack is available via the BDA website.

Summing Up

It is important that the correct school is identified for your child. Although a school is on your doorstep, it may not always be the best one for your child's special needs. Visit all the schools in your area and see what specialist provision they can offer.

There are many private centres around which can provide access to extra tuition on a regular weekly basis. You may like to supplement your child's education with this or with private tutors. Both can help tremendously.

Chapter Fifteen

Health Problems

There are many medical reasons for students failing at school. The most obvious is if they cannot see or hear properly, as they will not be able to read/ write or respond appropriately. If you suspect your child may have a problem, this should be checked immediately. Your doctor or health visitor will be able to arrange for a medical or hearing test. Your local optometrists will carry out a full eye test, even with very young children.

There are many health problems that could affect your child at school. A few are listed below:

- General poor health and Inadequate diet, i.e., (lack of vitamins etc. see chapter 18).

- Deafness.

- Temporary deafness (glue ear).

- Visual problems

- Visual stress (light sensitivity) and dyslexia.

General poor health

This section does not really need explanation. A child needs to be fit and healthy to access the school curriculum. If you are concerned about your child for any reason you can ask your health visitor or doctor for advice.

Vitamins and health

We know that if children do not have a well-balanced diet of vitamins and minerals, it will show up with ill health. The government still says that we get all our vitamins and minerals from our food so there is no need to take pills.

As we spend so much time rushing around, grabbing processed and frozen meals, it may be that our children are missing out on the vital vitamins they need not only to grow but also to develop their mental capacities.

For further information on vitamins and supplements see chapter 18.

Arranging a medical

If the school is concerned that your child is not performing as well as he should be, they will ask for an Assessment of Educational Needs; part of the assessment will include a medical. The medical is usually carried out in your own home so you can express any concerns you have with the doctor in private.

Deafness in children

There are almost ten million people with a permanent hearing loss in the UK; approximately 35,000 of these are children. Many more experience temporary hearing problems in early childhood.

Deafness is often associated with older people but many children are born deaf or profoundly deaf – others become so after an illness. One million children (0 to eight years) will experience temporary deafness caused by glue ear. If this starts to impact on the child's education, it may come under a condition known as 'acquired dyslexia'. Acquired dyslexia does not mean it has to be permanent.

Temporary Deafness – Glue ear

This is a common condition in childhood. Most children will get glue ear at some stage in their lives; it usually clears up very quickly. The tube becomes obstructed by adenoids at the back of the nose so air cannot enter the middle ear and the cavity fills with fluid. The eardrum becomes dark looking and, as time goes on, the fluid becomes thicker until it has the consistency of thick glue. Often the only sign is deafness. Children's schooling may suffer and behaviour may deteriorate.

In a lot of cases it will clear by itself, but in severe cases treatment will involve making a small hole in the drum, usually under a general anaesthetic. A tube (grommet) may be inserted and the adenoids may be removed. Adenoids usually disappear at puberty and most children with glue ear do not need treatment after this time. The hearing is usually restored to normal.

Checking your child's hearing – the Newborn Hearing Screening Programme (NHSP)

In the UK, the Newborn Hearing Screening Programme, which started in 2005, offers all new parents the opportunity to have their baby's hearing screened within the first few weeks of birth. If you think there may still be a problem you can ask your health visitor to arrange for further testing to be carried out. Some schools employ a school nurse so a child's hearing may be routinely checked once they start school.

Pardon! What did you say?

If your child cannot hear properly, it may be causing his problems. However, there may be a simple remedy that can correct the problem almost immediately. Wax in the ear canal is the most common problem.

Wax is made normally but becomes a problem if excessive amounts are produced. It forms into small beads, mixes with dust and dead skin and falls out of the ear. This cleaning mechanism works well for most people and does not need any additional help, e.g., with cotton tipped sticks or fingers, etc.

'If students cannot see or hear properly, they will not be able to read/ write or respond appropriately.'

However, some people make abnormal amounts of wax and may have to have it removed by a doctor or nurse.

Where can I get help?

Action on Hearing Loss is the new name for the RNID (Royal National Institute for Deaf People) which is the largest charity representing the nine million both deaf and hard of hearing people in the UK. It campaigns for improvements in facilities and services, and for more awareness of deafness by both government bodies and members of the public. It also campaigns in particular for integrated schooling (where applicable) and encourages greater public awareness of these problems.

National Deaf Children's Society (NDCS)

NDCS is the national charity dedicated to working with deaf children and young people. Half of all deaf children are born deaf and half become deaf in their early years. In 2008, nearly three quarters of deaf children failed to achieve the government benchmark of five GCSEs at grades A*-C, including English and Maths.

Do deaf children have to attend a special school?

A large percentage of deaf children attend ordinary mainstream schools. Many of them receive additional special education support within their schools.

Deaf/Blind

There are currently 23,000 children who are deaf and blind in the UK.

Visual Problems

Visual problems are one of the most common causes of disability in the world. In Britain around two million people have sight problems – approximately 24,000 of these are children.

Most parents visit their doctor and dentist regularly, yet many of them still do not appreciate the importance of taking their children to the optometrists. (Until recently many people called them opticians.)

The Optical Information Council has estimated that one child in five may have undetected visual problems, yet half of all parents with children under eight have never taken their children for an eye test. Regular eye tests, using new techniques, may prevent children with learning difficulties from being labelled problem children and would enable them to be identified at a much earlier age. It is imperative that these tests are carried out before the child starts to fail, as the damage caused to their self-esteem is very difficult to restore.

Your local optometrists can test your child. This test is available in the UK under the NHS and is free for children under 16 (19 if they are in full-time education).

By having regular check-ups (at least every two years), optometrists can pick up undetected visual problems. The majority of children will have perfectly healthy eyes but some may not be able to focus properly, leading to learning difficulties. These problems can be remedied by spectacles and therefore sorted out very quickly.

In recent years, glasses have often been used as a 'fashion statement', making it much easier for children to select glasses they like and to not feel the 'odd one out'.

However, if there is a more serious problem which the orthoptic feels needs further investigation, they can refer your child to the orthoptic department at your local hospital.

Where can I get help with general sight loss?

The Royal National Institute for the Blind (RNIB) provides a practical service to help people get on with their lives. Their aim is to give blind and partially-sighted children the best possible start in life. With the right help, these children can perform as well as any other youngsters. They also campaign for integrated schooling (where applicable) and encourage greater public awareness of these problems.

Visual stress (light sensitivity) and dyslexia

Many people suffer from visual stress without being aware of it. Sometimes with children, it is only when the problem has been corrected that the child often says they thought that everyone saw letters, fuzzy or jumping about. One 12-year-old child said to me, 'All the words have jumped back into the right places.' He then went on to read as if he had been doing so for years. Other people describe headaches, blurred vision and letters 'running into each other'. These problems have often been called, Mears-Irlen syndrome, Intuitive Colorimeter, Scotopic sensitivity, Irlen syndrome and Visual stress syndrome and are all words used to explain a very similar problem.

These specialists can use a variety of screening tests and assessments, including:

■ Cerium coloured overlays

■ Visual stress syndrome (ViSS).

■ Mears-Irlen' syndrome, Intuitive Colorimeter

■ Harris Filters

■ Vision training (see chapter 16).

■ Dunlop Test (see chapter 16).

Coloured overlays and tinted glasses

Coloured overlays seem to work by filtering out light that causes distortions to print. The problems appear to be worse with black print on white paper. Students often report problems with eyestrain, migraine, etc.

Your child may benefit from glasses or lenses if when reading they find:

■ Letters merge together.

■ Letters appear in the wrong order.

■ Twirling letters.

■ Words are fuzzy.

- Words jump about.
- Difficulties in reading and keeping their place.
- Excessive rubbing and blinking of their eyes.
- Words appear as a jumbled puzzle.
- Words appear faded.

What can I do if my child has a problem?

If you suspect your child may have this problem, you can use a quick and simple screening test using Cerium overlays (coloured sheets). These overlays are clear coloured plastic sheets that are placed over written work. When the overlays are placed over text, many students say 'the words have stopped jumping about'. You can get these sheets in different colours and if you find they help then you can organise a full test at the optometrists using the Intuitive Colorimeter or Harris Filters. Crossbow have coloured 'Reading Rulers (Duo)' which are brilliant! Students don't feel conspicuous when using this ruler.

Coloured overlays have been shown to increase a child's reading speed on the *Rate of Reading Test' by more than 25% in some 5% of schoolchildren aged 7 to 8 years of age.

Cerium A4 coloured overlays

Cerium A4 coloured overlays and the full Cerium Coloured Overlays Testing Kit are both available from The Dyslexia Shop.

Lucid ViSS – (Visual Stress Assessment Pack)

This assessment pack can help identify people who experience visual stress. The complete Visual Stress Assessment Pack consisting of overlays and test kit, can be purchased through the Dyslexia Shop or Crossbow Education.

* Rate of Reading Test published by 'ioo Marketing'.

Arnold Wilkins, has an excellent book on this subject, called, *Reading Through Colour*.

If your child proves to have a problem using the Coloured Overlays, then he can have a full assessment using the Intuitive Colorimeter (see below).

What is an Intuitive Colorimeter?

The Intuitive Colorimeter was developed by Professor Arnold Wilkins and the Medical Research Council. It uses up to 7,000 different tints to measure exactly which colour helps individual students to read better. Glasses are then made for students to use with reading and writing. Research has shown that if a child uses coloured overlays, his reading speed increases and he has fewer headaches.

Headlines like 'Experts hail cure for child dyslexia' and 'A miracle cure' have appeared in many national newspapers. And they have all been talking about the wonderful success being achieved by scores of dyslexic students. The remarkable achievements have occurred after being prescribed vision training or tinted glasses. If the student finds a benefit with the colour, then glasses can be made or soft tinted lenses.

While the 'miracle cure' may have helped some children with this particular problem, it will obviously not help all children, but it is worth trying.

Where can I get this test?

There are still only a few optometrists who have the Intuitive Colorimeter on their premises. The test is not available on the NHS at the moment. For a full list of participating optometrists, check out my website, www.dyslexiaa2z.com and go to the health section.

Harris Filters

Dr David Harris has been researching ways of helping children with dyslexia since 1996. His award-winning Filter technology has been demonstrated to achieve dramatic and immediate results. Harris' range of special lenses that were originally developed to improve colour perception in the colour-blind are now making great strides with dyslexic students.

What are Harris Filters?

The majority of dyslexics have nerve fibres that transmit important information inefficiently between the eyes and the brain. This can result in poor control of eye movements and therefore increased difficulty with reading and understanding, loss of place on the line of text and poorer comprehension. Harris' special lenses reduce or eliminate visual perceptual distortions, a condition that affects reading ability in almost 74% of dyslexia sufferers.

Harris Filters can't make dyslexia completely disappear from an individual but it is claimed, they can help to improve performance and make reading easier. For further information, please contact the Harris Foundation's website or telephone: 0845 230 1771.

Chronically Sick and Disabled Persons Act

If you or your child has a hearing, sight loss or suffers with visual stress, they may have rights under the Chronically Sick and Disabled Persons Act (1970). You or they are almost certainly will have rights under the new Equality Act (see chapter 20.) This means that local authorities have a duty to provide services to people with disabilities.

Before you can receive help, your child will need to have his needs correctly assessed. Contact your local social services for further information. The relevant social worker or doctor can arrange an assessment. If your child is assessed as requiring a service, the authority has a duty to provide it (although they may charge for this service). For more information contact your local Disability Service.

If the local authority refuses to provide a service, you have every right to complain. In the first instance you should complain to the council itself (they all have complaints procedures in place so ask for a copy of them). If you do not have any success, contact the Citizens Advice Bureau or local government ombudsman for assistance.

Summing Up

If your child is suffering from a medical problem, it stands to reason that he may not be able to hear/see what is being said, especially if he sits at the back of the classroom. Ensure that all medical checks have been carried out and then you will have peace of mind.

Chapter Sixteen

Role of the Orthoptist in Assessing Children with Specific Learning Difficulties

By Christine Robinson (Mrs) DBO, SRO.

Children with specific learning difficulties may sometimes need to be referred to the orthoptist for a Dunlop Test. The tests carried out by the orthoptist help to analyse whether there are any contributory visual problems associated with the learning difficulties. Orthoptists are well qualified to undertake the testing of your child when there are specific learning difficulties. They are specially trained therapists who, among other things, assess vision for close work and distance and binocular function (how well the two eyes work together).

'Orthoptists do not promise a miraculous cure if treatment is undertaken, but it may improve the visual information processing which can cause great problems for these children.'

Some orthoptists have a special interest in assessing children with specific learning difficulties. They do not promise a miraculous cure if treatment is undertaken, but it may improve the visual information processing which can cause great problems for these children. Most of the children will still need specialised teaching.

How do I arrange referral to an orthoptist?

NHS referrals require a letter of introduction from your GP or the school doctor. Some orthoptists are happy to see private patients and in this instance a referral letter from your GP is not always essential. It is advisable to check the availability of these tests in your area as not all orthoptic departments are able to undertake this work.

What will the testing involve?

The Dunlop Test is one small part of your child's orthoptic assessment. The orthoptist will usually take a full case history, including details of any past treatment for eye problems.

The tests will include:

- Tests to eliminate the presence of a squint that causes 'cross eyes'.

- Checking of eye movements and ability to scan and pursue a moving target.

- Assessing the ability of the two eyes to look in together at a near point – i.e. convergence.

- Assessing the ability of both eyes to focus clearly on print at a near point, i.e. accommodation.

- Tests on stereoscopic vision – i.e. 3D vision.

- Tests on the reserves of muscle ability present to maintain comfortable use of both eyes together.

- The Dunlop Test – to determine whether there is a reference eye well established.

- Assessment with a selection of intuitive coloured overlays, if considered appropriate. If the child thinks one of the overlays helps, a rate of reading test is undertaken both with and without the choice filter.

- Assessment with the Dyslexia Research Trust's yellow and blue filters can also be given if considered appropriate.

The Dunlop Test

This test originated in Australia in 1971 and was designed by Mrs P. Dunlop, an orthoptist. Much research has been conducted in this country by Dr J. Stein, a physiologist, and Mrs S. Fowler, an orthoptist (Royal Berkshire Hospital, Reading).

The test involves looking into a special machine at pictures that help us to decide which eye is in charge of sending a message (in the form of a picture) to the language centre in the brain so the picture can be deciphered (i.e. into a word).

It is a two-eyed test – both eyes are open – and we learn whether a reference or lead eye is established.

This should not be confused with a dominant eye, which is tested when you hold a tube or kaleidoscope to one eye – invariably the other eye is automatically closed.

Will treatment be needed?

Once the tests are completed, your orthoptist will be able to discuss the findings with you.

If the vision is reduced, your child will need to see an optician or ophthalmologist (specialist eye doctor) to check that the eyes are healthy, and to have glasses ordered if necessary.

If there is no reference eye and the child is over seven, special glasses with one lens frosted over may be prescribed for all reading, writing and number work. This is not a self-help treatment and progress will need to be monitored carefully by your orthoptist. If your child already has a fixed reference eye then it is unlikely that frosted glasses will be needed.

Sometimes children with dyslexia need eye exercises to improve the accurate use of both eyes together at a near point. Indeed, they often admit that the words and letters move about or go fuzzy – they may not have commented on this as they think everyone else sees things in the same way!

If the intuitive coloured overlays are helpful, the child can be referred to an optometrist with a 'colorimeter' – this is a machine to determine the exact colour to be dispensed in tinted glasses. The advantage of glasses is that they can be used for writing as well as reading.

If a Dyslexia Research Trust filter is chosen, tinted glasses can be offered on loan for either of these colours.

Aims of treatment

- To develop a reference eye.
- To have a good ability to look in to a near point with both eyes together, and maintain a clear picture (convergence and accommodation).
- To have good smooth eye movements in scan and pursuit.
- To have good muscle reserves (fusional ability).

How long will treatment last?

If treatment is recommended, it could be as little as one month for exercises or up to a maximum of one year if frosted glasses are prescribed.

If a reference eye does not become established after a maximum of one year, treatment will be stopped.

If treatment is suggested, it is certainly worth a try as there is nothing to lose and it may prove to be extremely beneficial.

Christine Robinson (Mrs) DBO, SRO.
Senior orthoptist, Great Western Hospital, Swindon.

'If the brain has to "use up" concentration and energy in order to simply move the eyes along a line of print, then there is less likelihood that the contents of the text will have any meaning, that it will be remembered.'

Optometric evaluation

By Keith Holland, B.Sc, FBCO, DCLP

In order to be able to concentrate, absorb information and maintain interest in the written word, the visual system of a young person has been developed with certain capabilities. The eyes have to be capable of moving smoothly and easily along a line of print, jumping back and down to the beginning of the next line and repeating this action for extended periods of time.

Students also have to be able to adjust the focus of their eyes rapidly from distance to near and back again when copying from a blackboard.

Conscious or subconscious?

It is important that these activities can be performed without conscious thought or effort. If the brain has to 'use up' concentration and energy in order to simply move the eyes along a line of print, then there is less likelihood that the contents of the text will have any meaning, that they will be remembered or that the words which are coming next are anticipated. Reading has to become a subconscious action.

Learning to read

Learning to move the eyes in a way which enables us to read efficiently is like changing gear – it's a learned action. Some young people fail to develop this skill and as a result their reading and writing ability is often lower than expected.

Other skills such as ball catching or graceful gymnastic body movements can also be affected, and children with poorly developed vision systems are frequently observed to be clumsy and ill coordinated.

Behaviour optometry

Some fully qualified and state registered optometrists now additionally practise what is called behaviour optometry. Behaviour optometrists operate on the basis that visual skills are learned and therefore trainable.

Vision is considered to be an inseparable part of the whole human system and should not be regarded as a separate and individual function. This means that our behaviour and our environment can influence the way in which our visual system works, and vice versa.

Behavioural optometrists use activities and training to improve the efficiency of the whole visual system.

Vision training

Vision training or vision therapy provides a means of learning to use the visual system in a more efficient manner. When the visual system works more efficiently, more information can be received, processed and understood. When there are problems with visual perception and understanding vision input, achieving full potential can be helped by using the techniques of vision training.

This involves developing good body bilaterality, hand-eye coordination, form perception, directionality and visualisation skills, as well as ensuring that the muscles which focus and direct the eyes are functioning efficiently. Should vision training be necessary, these terms will become more meaningful as the therapy programme progresses.

Who can benefit?

Students with good visual abilities read faster with less effort, understand more of what they read and retain it longer. Athletes who use their vision effectively see things more quickly, more accurately and show good overall performance. The improvement in the processing of visual information can benefit many areas of life, especially at school, in sports and at work.

Optometric vision training is individually programmed to the specific needs of each patient, with the basic universally needed skills being included in all programmes. Other activities are designed to meet specific needs.

What to look for

Children who may benefit from vision training can often be seen when reading to have difficulty in keeping their place and in following lines of print.

Typically, a child will read with a finger or a marker under the line being read, and as they read they will move the whole of the head rather than simply following the print with their eyes. In many cases, mathematical ability and intelligence may be normal or higher than normal for the age, yet reading presents a problem.

The concentration span of a young person with a poorly developed visual system will often be very short. Time spent reading will come to an abrupt halt and a sudden complete lack of interest.

Who can help?

Obviously if a child has learning difficulties, all avenues of possible help have to be explored. In order to establish if there may be a visual component to the learning difficulty, a full eye examination must be carried out by an optometrist.

If it is suspected that there may be a developmental visual problem (in other words, all the bits are there and are healthy but are not coordinating properly), then your optometrist may wish to deal with this himself. Alternatively, you may choose to be referred to a behavioural optometrist who has more experience in helping with learning problems.

Where to go

The British Association of Behavioural Optometrists maintain a register of all optometrists who have attended a further education course specifically designed to develop their knowledge and skills.

'The concentration span of a young person with a poorly developed visual system will be often very short, and time spent reading will come to an abrupt halt and a sudden complete lack of interest.'

Summing Up

The Dunlop Test and vision training have often seemed to be surrounded in mystery, but quite simply means fully testing the eyes and training them to respond to appropriate treatment. This treatment may take a few months or several years. If successful, it can be a tremendous help to the child. These tests are usually carried out in optometrist departments in hospitals rather than at your local opticians.

Chapter Seventeen

Education is Compulsory – Not School

The majority of children in the UK go to school. However, they do not have to. It is education that is compulsory, not actually attending a school. If a child does not go to school in the UK, it is usually known as 'education otherwise' or 'home education'. While it is difficult to ascertain exactly how many children do not go to school in the UK, figures of around *100,000 (approximately 1%) of compulsory educational age children (2011) are being home educated. This figure is only going to increase because of the appalling state of education in our schools today.

*Home Education in the UK, website: www.home-education.org.uk

The law says that it is a parent's duty to cause their child to receive efficient full-time education suitable to his age, ability and aptitude, and to any special educational needs he may have, either by regular attendance at school or otherwise (Sylvia Jeffs 1996).

There are many reasons why some children do not go to school. Some of these include the following:

- Parents simply do not want to 'let go' of their children.
- Parents believe they can educate their children better than the state.
- Some parents believe if they have a gifted child, they can provide a better education than at their local school.

- Children with special needs need more attention than is available at some schools.

- Some schools have failed their children.

- Some children refuse to go to school.

- Some children are being bullied.

- Sometimes special dietary needs cannot be met at school.

- The child has been expelled.

- Religious reasons.

- The child is chronically ill.

If a child is already registered at a school, he must be de-registered in accordance with the Pupil's Registration Regulations. The parents must write to the head teacher to explain that they are home-educating, i.e. have already started teaching.

This is an automatic procedure for children at mainstream schools: after the headteacher receives written notification from the parent, he will notify the LEA.

Contrary to popular belief you do not need:

- Permission to educate your child outside school.

- To justify your decision.

- To inform the LEA (there are sometimes exceptions).

- To hold teaching qualifications.

- To follow the national curriculum.

- To follow a specific syllabus.

- To follow a timetable.

- To follow school hours.

- To have formal school-type lessons.

Many LEAs are quite supportive of children being educated at home (unlike years ago) and offer valuable help, advice and equipment.

'The majority of children in the UK go to school. However, they do not have to. It is education that is compulsory, not actually attending a school.'

Education Otherwise is a leading organisation in helping and explaining people's rights to education at home. They have campaigned for higher recognition for many years. They have a wide range of books and booklets which explain your rights and duties and discuss the practicalities of dealing with educational authorities. Another useful organisation is Home Education, which has very good information on legal issues and an extensive information on educating at home.

Summing Up

We normally think that education is carried out only in schools, but for a variety of reasons there are a percentage of children who are educated outside these establishments. At all times we must remember that it is the parent's choice and not the LEA's.

It is the education that is compulsory, not school.

Chapter Eighteen

Vitamins and Health

Most people would accept the premise that eating a balanced diet is essential to our children's mental and physical development. Many scientific studies have shown that a nutritionally complete diet is necessary in the development of vision, learning ability and coordination. But are our children getting a well-balanced diet or should they be taking supplements? Can taking supplements of fatty acids, zinc and iron cure dyslexia, dyspraxia and ADHD? Many parents who use these supplements say a resounding 'yes', and there now appears to be strong evidence to support this.

One study indicated that children who had a decent breakfast before exams performed much better than those who skipped breakfast or just had a bowl of cereal. Another study showed that if a student ate a Mars bar directly before an exam, they also performed better (this is the only time I encouraged my boys to eat Mars bars). The most likely reason for these results is that the breakfast/chocolate provides a short-lived surge in blood glucose levels so brain functioning improves within a short period of time.

Fatty acids

There have been a multitude of studies over the last decade, which concluded that abnormal levels of fatty acids in the brain could be behind the practical and behavioural problems experienced by 'developmental dyslexic' children, as well as those with dyspraxia and ADHD. (There is further information on the link between fatty acids and ADHD in chapter 8.)

Many parents of dyslexic, dyspraxic and ADHD children now give their children these supplements – some parents have seen remarkable results.

When I worked at the Swindon Dyslexia Centre, many of the parents attending said that within a very short period of time their child was calmer, could concentrate better and had started to catch up with his reading and writing. This does not appear to help everyone but is certainly worth trying.

Michael – nine years

Dyslexic and ADHD

Can taking supplements of fatty acids, zinc and iron cure dyslexia, dyspraxia and ADHD? Many parents who use these supplements say a resounding "yes".'

Michael has dyslexia and ADHD. He had severe literacy problems and found it difficult to concentrate and sit still for long.

Michael attended the Swindon Dyslexia Centre twice a week to help him with his problems. While they were there one day, his mother read an article on Efalex. She said she was desperate and 'willing to try anything'. Within weeks of Michael taking the tablets, she noticed a difference in his behaviour at home. The school also commented on his improvement in concentration span and behaviour.

Michael is now making steady progress with reading, writing and spelling, and can sit still for much longer periods.

His mother said, 'It is truly remarkable, certainly worth the money.'

How long does it take for the fatty acids to work?

It can take up to three months for the fatty acids to be effective, so you usually have to start on a higher dose and then reduce them.

Two of the products containing fatty acids are:

- Efalex (liquid or tablets). Efamol, the makers of 'Efalex', say their product 'is the only fatty acid formula that has been clinically proven to relieve symptoms of learning and behaviour disorders such as dyslexia, dyspraxia and attention deficit hyperactivity disorder'. Efalex provides the important long chain fatty acids, DHA and AA, needed to help maintain eye and brain function and the development of vision.

Need2Know

- Equazen eye q (soft chews). This contains the long chain polyunsaturated fatty acids, EPA and DHA . Also included is GLA from EPA-rich marine oil and pure evening primrose oil. Long chain polyunsaturated fatty acids play an important role in the development of the eye and brain, especially vision, coordination, memory and concentration.

These supplements are now available as liquid, tablets or 'chews' which make them more palatable for children. They can be purchased from chemists, health shops and most large supermarkets.

Iron supplements

In a study published in November 1996, an American group of scientists said teenage girls improved if they were given iron supplements. Previous research appears to show that anaemia affects the mental abilities of children. Animal research has also hinted that iron deficiency is enough to change brain iron levels, which in turn alter the way neurotransmitters behave in the brain.

Zinc supplements

Zinc is one of our body's most important trace minerals and there has been some research to show that people with dyslexia have been linked to a deficiency of this mineral.

Zinc plays an important part in the body's immune system. A shortage can affect the healing process because the body is unable to store it, therefore it is vital that we eat enough zinc in our daily diet to stay healthy. An indicator of a lack of zinc includes white marks on fingernails and dandruff.

Zinc can be found in many foods, including:

- Lean meat.
- Liver.
- Cheddar cheese.
- Chicken.
- Eggs.

'Zinc is one of our body's most important trace minerals and there has been some research to show that people with dyslexia have been linked to a deficiency of this mineral.'

- Wholemeal breads.
- Wholegrain cereals.
- Dried beans.
- Seafood.

Zinc can be destroyed or blocked by various things, including tannin (found in tea, coffee and alcohol), food colourings and additives.

Should we take supplements?

Most people agree that if our children eat a well-balanced diet there is no need to take supplements and they will be healthy and well. However, that is not always possible when we are rushing around, trying to be all things to everyone.

Supplements can be a safe and effective ways of ensuring children are getting the nutrients needed to help them keep healthy and aid their mood and concentration generally.

'Most people agree that if our children eat a well balanced diet there is no need to take supplements, and they will be healthy and well. However, that is not always possible when we are rushing around, trying to be all things to everyone.'

Summing Up

While the debate regarding vitamin supplements continues, the experts seem to disagree with each other constantly. Some argue that if our children receive a well-balanced diet, they do not need to take vitamin supplements. Others say that with vitamin supplements, children who are deficient in some areas of their diet will make faster progress.

Without any concrete evidence and guidance from the government, the decision has to be left to you.

Chapter Nineteen

Career Options

Further education/career choices

Thinking about career choices while still at school is extremely daunting for the student and the decision made at this stage may affect their whole working life. However, our experiences at school, college and in the workplace make us consider our career choices regularly throughout our working lives. These days it is unusual to have a job for life and we have to continue to change and develop our skills over the years.

Careers advice – Next Step (over 19's)

Next Step (used to be called careers offices) have offices all over the country and in many different locations, such as: job centres; libraries; community centres; health centres etc. Next Step can give advice to adults over 19. This advice is available over the phone, on the Internet or in 'face-to-face' interviews. (I telephoned them and asked them lots of different things, and I must admit they were extremely helpful.)

The Next Step website is also very good and easy to use. Useful sections:

- Finding out what you are good at, i.e. looks at your skills and abilities

- Searches through many different courses

- Has lots of information on planning your career.

- Has information on over 700 job roles such as, police workers, firefighters, teachers, care workers, gardeners, chefs etc.

- Has advice on how to present your curriculum vitae (CV)

'These days it is unusual to have a job for life and we have to continue to change over the years.'

- Can advise you on interviews, what to expect, how to dress etc.

- Has a section on free psychometric testing. (See section on psychometric testing later in this chapter.)

Job Centres

Job centres hold lots of information on hundreds of jobs available in your area and can give some general advice on jobs.

Careers advice – Connexions (Under 18s)

During the last two years at school, a careers adviser from Connexions will be available to talk to students. (These advisors will be based in most large schools from 2011.) Every student will have the opportunity of an in-depth interview with them. The interview will be centred on your child and will discuss his strengths, interests and ambitions. It will also explain the education and training options open to him. Your child may be offered the opportunity of carrying out psychometric testing. It is a very useful tool, which helps to see what your child is good at, or where his interests lie. Once this has been completed, a Careers Guidance Plan can then be developed which will summarise the meeting and the steps agreed.

The student will then have to make a decision about which way he would like to go:

 Further academic studies, e.g. A level or further GCSEs.

- Vocational course – work-related courses/GNVQs.

- Specific training or employment.

- Connexions also provide support up to the age of 25 if you have learning difficulties (such as dyslexia, and/or disabilities.

Assessment support at employment centres

All job centres have a registered person who is referred to as a disability employment adviser (DEA). This person is the 'gatekeeper' to specialist vocational support for people with disabilities. They will have a great deal of experience and, more importantly, understanding of people with learning difficulties in the work situation.

Dyslexia is a registered disability under the Chronically Sick and Disabled Persons Act 1970, Education Act 1993 the Disability Discrimination Act 1995 and the Equal Opportunities Act November 2010. All employment centres have been provided with a comprehensive description of dyslexia.

The Adult Literacy Service

The Adult Literacy Service works with your LEA and provides advice and information to students with learning disabilities. The Further Education Funding Council may be able to give additional funding to students with special educational needs. Colleges try to ensure that there are equal opportunities for all potential students.

Psychometric testing

Psychometric testing can help all students and is sometimes arranged in school in conjunction with the careers adviser. The testing includes comprehensive assessments that can be carried out in writing or on a computer. The tests provide an objective assessment of an individual's abilities and personality, matching them to possible career choices held on a computer. It analyses the student's personal information and interests, then suggests career choices they may not have thought of. There are many different types of tests around but they are all similar.

Is it worth having a psychometric test?

We spend between 25% and 33% of our time at work so it is very important to find a job you like. If your child chooses a career that does not suit them, they will soon become unhappy. No one wants a job they hate. So why not take the time to find a job that suits your personality?

Psychometric testing can help you find a job:

- You are suited to.
- Which gives you job satisfaction.
- That encourages you to contribute something to the success of the company.

These tests are also available in some libraries, colleges and educational establishments, in some private companies and online. Some of these are free for a short test and others charge for an in-depth test. Either way, they are worthwhile and sometimes come up with some interesting facts.

Some companies offer free online tests, usually have a very short introductory test and then you pay for a more in-depth one.

One company offering a free online test is: www.psychometricadvantage.co.uk.

Another company offers a free 'aptitude test' and 'personality test': www.jobtestprep.co.uk/freepsychometrics.aspx.

Next Step online have free in-depth tests and you can start at a basic level and move on to a higher one. These tests are brilliant!

Summing Up

A lot of help and advice is now given to students at school. This starts when the pupils are approximately 13-14 years of age and continues until they leave school. This ensures that the pupil has been given the option of different career choices available to them.

Psychometric testing is now widely available at some schools, colleges, universities, career offices and free online, and this can be used as a great tool for all of us and particularly if you have special needs.

Chapter Twenty

Dyslexia and the Equality Act 2010

The 'Equality Act' became law in October 2010, with the objectives of strengthening and clarifying existing discrimination law to support progress on equality issues. The Act harmonises and replaces most of the previous legislation (such as the Disability Discrimination Act 1995) and ensures consistency in what you need to do to make your workplace a fair environment and to comply with the law.

The Act, includes a new protection from discrimination arising from disability. This states that it is discrimination to treat a disabled person unfavourably because of something connected with their disability (e.g. a tendency to make spelling mistakes arising from dyslexia). This type of discrimination is unlawful where the employer or other person acting for the employer knows, or could reasonably be expected to know, that the person has a disability. This type of discrimination is only justifiable if an employer can show that it is a proportionate means of achieving a legitimate aim.

In order to get the best from your staff it is important that you understand exactly what dyslexia is. By understanding the condition you will be able to support your dyslexic employees.

How many of your staff and customers are dyslexic?

How many of your staff are dyslexic? Do you know what dyslexia is and how you can make 'reasonable adjustments' to help those who are dyslexic? By understanding what dyslexia is you will be able to support your dyslexic employees. Sometimes just minor adjustments in the workplace can make it easier for your staff. Dyslexia affects 10% of the population. Therefore this is likely to have an impact, not just on your staff, but also on 10% of your customers, suppliers and delivery people, indeed everyone you come into contact with!

What is dyslexia?

Dyslexia affects 10% of the population, 4% severely. Problems can show themselves in reading, writing, number work, short-term memory, hand control and visual processing. Timekeeping, sense of direction and interpersonal skills can also be affected.

Many people with dyslexia are extremely bright in lots of ways, always talking and asking questions, but they do not seem to reach their full potential in the academic field. (For a full description on dyslexia, please see chapter 3.)

What is a user-friendly workplace?

Trying to create a 'user-friendly' workplace is good practice. Many dyslexics do not need a lot of adjustments to their working environment but often small changes can really help. Many of these changes are simple and inexpensive.

As an employer you can help by:

- Letting prospective employees apply online for job applications.
- Making application forms easy. (Why not get a dyslexic employee to help design/change one or ask for help from a dyslexia charity?)
- Using computer typeface in a font like Arial 12 to help make things easier to read.
- Using pastel coloured paper wherever possible.

'Many people with dyslexia are extremely bright in lots of ways, always talking and asking questions, but they do not seem to reach their full potential in the academic field.'

- Highlighting important information in documents.

On computers:

- Consider whether a laptop or 'tablet' would be more suitable for the employee.

- Make sure you can change the background colour on the screen.

- Encourage the employee to make the font size larger if it will help.

- Use speech-to-text software.

- Ensure there are spelling and grammar checkers installed.

- Use reminders on computers for important meetings, etc.

Other gadgets include:

- Electronic organisers.

- Palmtop computers.

- Dictaphones.

- Tape recorders.

- Talking calculators – excellent for people with number problems.

Generally in the workplace:

- Use voice mail rather than memos.

- Keep the room quiet and away from distractions.

- Use large boards above desks to remind employees of important dates.

If additional costs are required, such as a voice-activated computer, the employer can apply for funding through the government's Access to Work (AtW) scheme.

Equality Act – What's new for employers?

The Equality Act replaces previous legislation (such as the Disability Discrimination Act) and ensures consistency in what you need to do to make your workplace a fair environment and to comply with the law. 'Equality Act – What's new for employers', is a useful guide to help individuals and companies understand what discrimination issues mean and looks at employees' rights.

ACAS also offer training courses for companies. They offer hands-on useful support to help you with your business.

Further information is available on the ACAS website www.acas.org.uk.

Code of Practice for Employers

The British Dyslexia Association 'Code of Practice for Employers' is a guide for employers on supporting employees with dyslexic difficulties. It includes guidance on recruitment, written tests, assessments, 'reasonable adjustments' and an employer's obligations under the Equality Act.

This is an invaluable publication for all employers, particularly HR, Personnel and Occupational Health departments etc.

The guide is available from the BDA priced £10 plus p&p. A PDF version is available.

Access to Work Scheme (AtW)

The Access to Work Scheme (AtW) is operated through your local JobCentre Plus office. Access to Work can help you if your health or disability affects the way you do your job. It gives you and your employer advice and support with extra costs which may arise because of your needs.

Do I need to have an Assessment?

You may need to have an occupational health assessment carried out. This can be arranged via the local health authority (LHA) or under the Access to Work scheme. The assessment will then identify and recommend areas to enable the dyslexic employee to benefit in the workplace. (You do not need to prove you are dyslexic, however, it is useful to be assessed as it identifies the precise help you need.)

Once a need is identified, the Access to Work scheme can pay for part of the adjustments. Employers (company bosses) are required to share part of the cost with the AtW by paying between £300 to a £1000, plus a further minimum 20% of the cost up to £10,000. (Small companies, with less than nine employees will not be expected to pay anything.) Some companies may be able to offset this cost against tax.

After a year, Access to Work, will review your circumstances, to see whether you need any additional support.

Can I get support from the Access to Work scheme?

Access to Work will pay 100% of the approved costs if you are:

- Self-employed.
- Unemployed and starting a new job.
- Working for an employer and have been in a job for less than six weeks.
- Have people changing jobs in your company.

Whatever the employment status, Access to Work will also pay 100% of the approved costs of help with:

- Support workers.
- Fares to work.
- Communicator support at interview.

In all these cases the employer orders the products listed by the Access to Work scheme, and pays for them. They then claim the amount back off Access to Work. This scheme may be able to pay for equipment, adapting premises or for a support worker.

Can I get a form to see if I can get support?

On the DirectGov, website, you can download a form to see if you are eligible for Access to Work support. If you fit the criteria you can print a confirmation letter and give it to your employer or prospective employers. Further information van be obtained from DirectGov, Access to Work Scheme, or from your local jobcentre.

Occupational health assessments

An occupational health assessment can be carried out by your local health authority or under the Access to Work scheme.

There are several types of tests available:

- Occupational health assessment.
- Dyslexia screening assessment (but you do not have to prove you are dyslexic).
- Educational psychologist's report.

These assessments are very useful because it may be that the employee has never been identified as dyslexic, and the report would be able to identify specific work areas that would help him.

Where can I get further information?

The organisations below can send you further information.

- For information on the Right to Work (RtW) scheme contact your local JobCentre Plus office.

- For a leaflet to see if you are eligible to get support under the Access to Work scheme, go online and visit www.direct.gov.uk, search for 'Access to Work scheme' or write to Disability on the Agenda.

For information on the Equality Act, go online and visit www.direct.gov.uk and type in 'protected characteristics'.

- The British Dyslexia Association (BDA) has an information pack available, 'Code of Practice for Employers', for £10.

See the help list at the back of the book for contact details.

Summing Up

As this is quite new legislation, it is obvious that not everyone will know what to do about all of the things mentioned previously. However, the British Dyslexia Association (BDA) has very useful information on dyslexia and employers, so does ACAS. There is no excuse for employers who do not to take up this offer, especially when they can get most of the 'reasonable adjustments' paid for.

Chapter Twenty-One

Legal Advice

Sometimes, when parents have tried everything to get the help they need for their child, things still do not work out. It is on these occasions when they feel there is absolutely nothing further to do that they may decide to seek legal help.

One former pupil, Ms Pamela Phelps, 26, successfully sued the London Borough of Hillingdon and was awarded over £46,000 because they failed to diagnose her dyslexia.

Another former pupil, Mr Robin Johnson, was awarded over £50,000 in compensation, plus costs, at Stockport County Court because his dyslexia went undetected by teachers for almost a decade. Johnson said he did not reach his full potential at school, because he was let down during his early school days. With these type of monies, being paid out by local authorities, it is really in their interests to sort problems out before they intensify to this level.

There are specialist firms offering legal advice to people who have had difficulties, for whatever reason, with their LEAs, colleges, etc. When looking for a company, please ensure the legal firms are registered with the Education Law Association. The Law Society regulates these associations.

These companies can usually provide legal representation on all aspects of education law, including:

- Information about assessments and statementing.
- Statementing procedures.
- Enforcement of statements.
- Special educational needs.

'Pamela Phelps, 26, successfully sued the London Borough of Hillingdon and was awarded over £46,000 because they failed to diagnose her dyslexia.'

- Special educational needs tribunals.
- Admission to schools you have chosen.
- Dealing with a school that wants to reduce the teaching time/therapy for your child.
- Finding suitable experts for diagnosis of your child's needs.
- Advice regarding provision from the LEA or school.
- Independent school placements.
- Exclusion.
- School refusals.
- Dealing with bullying.
- Home tuition.
- Help for students whose schools have failed them.

Chapter Twenty-Two

Help and Resources

Setting up a support group

I receive hundreds of calls each year asking how you go about setting up a support group.

It is not difficult at all. We all need help and support at some time or another. When your child has special needs, it is easy to feel as if you are the only one in the world with difficulties. There are thousands of children who have problems with their education. Parents need to come together to talk their problems through – to help and advise each other. Your problem will not be a new one. If you are suffering because of it, you can bet there are others out there in the same position.

Why not set up a support group?

Why not form a support group in your area? It isn't as hard as you may think! If you need support, there must be others feeling the same. Don't wait until someone else does it – because they might not!

How do I go about it?

Ask other parents to see if they are interested in joining.

'Your problem will not be a new one. If you are suffering because of it, you can bet there are others out there in the same position.'

- Visit your local library, Citizens Advice Bureau or other voluntary agencies to see if they have any information that may help you.

- Ask yourself, what exactly is needed in your area?

- Do you want to have meetings every week/month?

- Where will your meetings be? (It might be best to hold the first meeting in a local hall.)

- Contact the national charity to see what help they can offer.

- Try to get a guest speaker for your first meeting from a national organisation.

Ask other parents to give you a hand. If you don't ask, you don't get; that is my maxim – you can't do everything yourself! It may seem hard at the start but keep going – it gets easier.

Advertising your group

No, I don't mean by paying for advertisements with the local press. My company does not have an advertising budget at all. The local radio and newspapers need local news – let them know what you are doing. Just contact them by email, letter or telephone. Don't forget local news is their business!

Press release

The quickest way to let the press know is by a press release. Don't panic. This is very easy. It is just like writing a letter and then taking out all the chitchat, leaving just the bones. Something similar to the example opposite will be sufficient.

Maria Chivers

1 Any Road

Any Town

Any County

0123 454678

Press Release

Dyslexia Support Group

There will be a meeting in West Drayton School Hall, on Wednesday 17th November at 7.30, to discuss the setting up of a support group for Dyslexia.

There will be a guest speaker from the British Dyslexia Association who will talk on 'Special Educational Needs – How you can help'.

The aim is to form a group for parents and carers, providing support and information about services in our area. There will be a small entrance fee of £1.00. Refreshments will be available.

For further information, please contact Maria Chivers.

Tel. 0123 454678.

****

Don't forget: if you need help, so do other people in the same situation!

And finally . . .

If we learn one thing from our research into dyslexia it is that early identification has got to be the key. Once you identify a child as having a learning difficulty and rule out any medical problems, you can start working towards a solution – before that child starts to fail!

I have been researching dyslexia for over 25 years and so I hope I have answered many of your questions about dyslexia and other learning difficulties. Unfortunately, there is no magic cure or secret formula, but there is a lot of help and advice available. I hope I have shown how you could use this to help your child. Check out my site on www.dyslexiaa2z.com for lots of information on dyslexia and other specific learning difficulties (SpLDs).

The British Dyslexia Association is 40 years old but there is still a need for more public and professional recognition of the problem. Voluntary groups, awareness weeks, conferences and the like all help to achieve this, and we can all support these. By joining the British Dyslexia Association you will receive up-to-date newsletters and information about the latest ideas in the dyslexia world. It is well worth a few pounds a year for membership – the stronger they are, the more they can get things changed in schools, colleges and the workplace.

I wish you all the best and good luck to you all.

Dyslexia A2Z.com

For all your dyslexia requirements, look at my website www.dyslexiaa2z.com.

Dyslexia A2Z has information on the following:

- Dyslexia assessments and tests.
- Dyscalculia (maths) assessments and tests.
- Dysgraphia (handwriting) assessments and tests.
- Dyslexia tutors.
- Psychologists.
- Alternative therapists.
- Complementary therapists.
- Irlen syndrome.
- Intuitive Colorimeter.
- Diet, vitamins, minerals and fatty acids.
- Books on dyslexia, dyscalculia, dysgraphia, etc.
- Specialist software.
- ChromaGen.
- Phono-Graphix.
- NLP.
- NDD.
- ARROW.

And more . . .

Don't Let Dyslexia Get You Down

More than 100 pupils from Seaford College in West Sussex, aged 10-18, have recorded a CD. The idea was to dispel some of the myths surrounding dyslexia, and the lyrics pay tribute to celebrities who have succeeded despite their learning difficulties.

The song has been written by the school's head of learning support, Nick Foster, with music composed and arranged by the school's head of RE, Richard Bailey.

Proceeds from the sale of the CDs will go towards two charities.

Don't let dyslexia get you down,
Look at the famous ones who have found
Their own dyslexia is no big deal,
And that is now how you can really feel.
Dyslexia's no big deal.

Don't let dyslexia get to you,
Look at the many things you can do.
The world won't stop if your spelling's not great.
Just use a spellchecker, or even dictate.
Have confidence and create.

Look at the great Albert Einstein,
What a genius, what a mind.
Charles Darwin – the first man to state that
Humans are descended from the ape.

Look at the great Winston Churchill
Who led this country with such skill.
Thomas Edison got it right,
Invented the bulb and gave us light.

Now who could be much sexier
Than Tom Cruise with dyslexia?
Whoopi Goldberg and the singer Cher,
Successful entertainers and millionaires.

Now Leonardo da Vinci
Earned his place in history,
A brilliant artist, an inventor too,
An exceptional man is the popular view.

He achieved success and you can do that too.

Help List

A2Z

www.dyslexiaa2z.com
This website was set up to help people find information on dyslexia in one place. Details on a wide range of things are included: teachers, psychologists, therapists, vitamins and supplements. (See page 195 for further details.)

ACAS

www.acas.org.uk
ACAS promote employment relations and HR excellence. They are an extremely helpful company for individual clients or companies.

Access to Work (Access2Work)

Access to Work
www.direct.gov.uk/en/DisabledPeople/Employmentsupport/
WorkSchemesAndProgrammes/DG_4000347
Advice on work-related issues.

ACE (Advisory Centre for Education Ltd)

United House, North Road, London, N7 9DP
Tel: 0808 800 5793
www.ace-ed.org.uk
Advice on education to parents and schools – produces a wide range of publications.

Action on Hearing Loss

19-23 Featherstone Street, London, EC1Y 8SL
Tel: 0808 808 0123
Textphone: 0808 808 900
www.rnid.org.uk
This leading charity campaigns for improvements in facilities and services.

ADO (Adult Dyslexia Organisation)

Ground Floor, Secker House, Minet Road, Loughborough Estate, London, SW9 7TP
Tel: 0207 924 9559
www.adult-dyslexia.org
The ADO offers information, support, counselling and advice. They also have a comprehensive guide on employment and dyslexia.

Anything Left-Handed

PO Box 344, Tadworth, KT20 9DL
Tel: 020 8770 3722
www.anythingleft-handed.co.uk
Information and hundreds of products for left-handers.

ARROW Tuition Ltd

Arrow Centre, Bridgwater College, Cannington Court, Cannington, Somerset, TA5 2HA
Tel: 01278 652863
www.self-voice.com

Arts Dyslexia Trust (ADT)

14 Churchfield Way, Wye, Ashford, Kent, TN25 5EQ
Tel: 01233 811960
www.artsdyslexiatrust.org

AVP

Angel House, Sherston, Malmesbury, Wiltshire, SN16 0LH
Tel: 01291 625 439
www.avp.co.uk
Specialist computer programs.

BABO (British Association of Behavioural Optometrists)

Tel: 01256 862547
www.babo.co.uk
Register of members who are verified as having met the requirements for continuing education in behaviour optometry.

Back in Action

www.backinaction.co.uk

A portable seat wedge that converts to a writing slope. See website for office telephone numbers.

Basic Skills Agency (now moved to NIACE)

Chetwynd House, 21 De Montfort Street, Leicester, LE1 7GE

Tel: 0116 204 4200

www.niace.org.uk

British Deaf Association

www.bda.org.uk

Contains the latest information about the deaf association and sign language. See the website for UK offices.

British Dyslexia Association

Unit 8, Bracknell Beeches, Old Bracknell Lane, Bracknell, RG12 7BW

Tel: 0845 251 9002

www.bdadyslexia.org.uk

Aims to advance education and employment opportunities for people with dyslexia. Advice available on identification, teaching, etc. Wide list of books, brochures and software available.

Bristol Dyslexia Centre

11 Upper Belgrave Road, Clifton, Bristol, BS8 2XH

Tel: 0117 973 9405

www.dyslexiacentre.co.uk

Specialist software 'Nessy' has been developed by the centre.

Calibre

Calibre Audio Library, Weston Turville, Aylesbury, Buckinghamshire, HP22 5XQ

Tel: 01296 432 339

www.calibre.org.uk

Books for coursework and examinations on tape.

Children's Legal Centre

University of Essex, Wivenhoe Park, Colchester, CO4 3SQ
Tel: 08088 020 008
www.childrenslegalcentre.com
A unique, independent national charity concerned with law and policy affecting children and young people.

Chronically Sick & Disabled Persons Act (CSDP)1970

www.legislation.gov
Government legislation regarding the 'Chronically Sick and Disabled Persons Act 1970'.

Citizens Advice Bureau (CAB)

115-123 Pentonville Road, London, N1 9LZ
Tel: 020 7833 2181 (admin only – no advice)
www.nacab.org.uk

CReSTeD (Council for the Registration of Schools Teaching Dyslexic Pupils)

Old Post House, Castle Street, Whittington, Shropshire, SY11 4DF
Tel: 0845 601 5013
www.crested.org.uk
CReSTeD maintain a Register of Schools for dyslexic children.

Department for Education (DFE)

www.education.gov.uk
Government department set up to assist parents and professionals with all aspects of education.

Directory of Social Change

Directory of Social Change, 24 Stephenson Way, London, NW 2DP
Tel: 020 7391 4800
www.dsc.org.uk
Independent source of information and support to voluntary and community sectors.

The Disability Discrimination Act (Changed to Equality Act)

Disability on the Agenda, Freepost, Bristol, BS38 7DE
www.disability.gov.uk

Dyscovery Centre

The Dyscovery Centre, Felthorpe House, Caerleon Campus, Lodge Road,
Caerleon, Newport, NP18 3QR.
Tel: 01633 432330
www.newport.ac.uk/research/researchcentres/Centres/Dyscovery%20Centre/
About/Pages/default.aspx
Provides a specialist and high quality service helping individuals with living and
learning difficulties.

Dyslexia Action

Head Office, Park House, Wick Road, Egham, Surrey, TW20 0HH
Tel: 01784 222 300
www.dyslexiaaction.org.uk
Main functions are assessment and tuition in their 26 centres, and teacher
training. They also carry out research and develop specialist teaching materials.

Dyslexia Association of Ireland

Suffolk Chambers, 1 Suffolk Street, Dublin 2, Ireland
Tel: 01 6790276
www.dyslexia.ie
Aims to promote awareness of SpLDs/dyslexia.

Dyslexia Research Trust

Dyslexia Research Trust, The Sherrington Building, Department of Physiology
Anatomy and Genetics, Parks Road,
Oxford, OX1 3PT.
www.dyslexic.org.uk
A wide range of information and research on dyslexia.

Dyslexia Shop, The

Tel: 01394 671 878

www.thedyslexiashop.co.uk

Hundreds of products on dyslexia including cerium overlays and screening kit. Very helpful company, run by Honor Paige and Linda.

Dyspraxia Foundation

8 West Alley, Hitchin, Hertfordshire, SG5 1EG

Tel: 01462 454 986 (10am-1pm, Mon-Fri.)

www.dyspraxiafoundation.org.uk

This registered charity offers help and advice on dyspraxia. Lots of publications available.

Education Otherwise

PO Box 3761, Swindon, SN2 9GT

www.education-otherwise.net

Provides support and information for families whose children are being educated outside school.

Educational Psychologists (Association of)

4 The Riverside Centre, Frankland Lane, Durham, DH1 5TA

Tel: 01913 849 512

www.aep.org.uk

Efamol Ltd (Efalex)

14, The Mole Business Park, Leatherhead, Surrey, KT22 7BA

www.efamol.com/

Suppliers of fatty acids.

Gamz

25 Albert Park Road, Malvery, Worcestershire, WR14 1HW

Tel: 01684 562 158

www.gamzuk.com

Great website and lots of literacy games for dyslexics and others.

Helen Arkell Dyslexia Centre

Arkell Lane, Frensham, Farnham, Surrey, GU10 3BW
Tel: 01252 792 400
www.arkellcentre.org.uk
A registered charity offering expert assessment and specialist tuition to anyone with dyslexia or other SpLDs.

(HESC) Health, Education and Social Care (formerly SENDIST)

The Special Educational Needs and Disability now sits in the Health, Education and Social Care (HESC) Chamber of the First-Tier Tribunal.
www.justice.gov.uk/guidance/courts-and-tribunals/tribunals/send/index.htm

Home Education or (Un-schooled)

Email: mike@home-education.org.uk
www.home-education.org.uk

Hyperactive Children's Support Group (HACSG)

Dept W, 71 Whyke Lane, Chichester, West Sussex, PO19 7PD
www.hacsg.org.uk

IANSYST Ltd

Fen House, Fen Road, Chesterton, Cambridge, CB4 1UN
Tel: 01223 420 101
www.iansyst.co.uk
Catalogue available for thousands of specialist equipment, including computer software, etc.

Independent Schools Council Information Services (ISCIS)

Independent Schools Council, St Vincent House, 30 Orange Street, London, WC2H 7HH
Tel: 020 7766 7070
www.isis.org.uk
Associations of independent schools in the UK.

IPSEA (Independent Panel for Special Education Advice)

Tel: 0800 018 4016

www.ipsea.org.uk

Gives free legally based advice to people about special educational needs.

Keith Holland Optometrist

27 St George's Road, Cheltenham, GL50 3DT

Tel: 01242 233 500

www.keithholland.co.uk

Award-winning specialist eye-care team in the treatment of children with learning disabilities.

Keytools (BigKeys)

Abacus House, 1 Spring Crescent, Southampton, SO17 2FZ

Tel: 023 8029 4500

www.keytools.co.uk

Range of inclusive computer access equipment for special needs.

LDA Living & Learning

Tel: 0845 120 4776

www.ldalearning.com

Wide selection of specialist software and products. Catalogue available.

Listening Books

12 Lant Street, London, SE1 1QH

Tel: 020 7407 9417

www.listening-books.org.uk

Members can choose from thousands of audiobooks to download to free to PCs, iPods or a large selection of portable devices. Books for coursework and examinations on tape. We help a wide range of organisations and individuals and provide our audiobooks on 3 easily accessible formats: through the post on CD, downloaded online and streamed from this website.

Local Government Ombudsman

See website for addresses.
Tel: 0300 061 0614
www.lgo.org.uk
Government ombudsman to look into complaints from people about various matters.

LUCID

3 Spencer Street, Beverley, East Yorkshire, HU17 9EG
Tel: 01482 882 121
www.lucid-research.com
Computerised testing equipment for dyslexia and visual stress.

Mensa Limited (British)

St John's House, St John's Square, Wolverhampton, WV2 4AH
Tel: 01902 772 771
www.mensa.org.uk

Mental Health Foundation

London Office: Colechurch House, 1 London Bridge Walk, London, SE1 2SX
Tel: 020 780 3 1100
Scotland Office: Merchants House, 30 George Square, Glasgow, G2 1EG.
Tel: 0141 572 0125
www.mhf.org.uk
Information service, leaflets and publications available.

National Association for the Gifted Child

NAGC, Suite 1-2, Challenge House, Sherwood Drive, Bletchley, Bucks, MK3 6DP
Tel: 01908 646 433
www.nagcbritain.org.uk
NAGC has newsletters and publications for the gifted child.

National Association for Special Educational Needs (NASEN)

Nasen House, 4/5 Amber Business Village, Amber Close, Amington, Tamworth, Staffs, B77 4RP
Tel: 01827 311 500
www.nasen.org.uk

National Blind Children's Society

Tel: 01278 764 764 (admin)
www.nbcs.org.uk

National Deaf Children's Society

15 Dufferin Street, London, EC1Y 8UR
Tel: 0808 800 8880
www.ndcs.org.uk
Helps families, parents and carers to maximise their skills and abilities.

National Federation of Access Centres (now National Network of Assessment Centres)

www.nnac.org
UK network of specialist services that work together to facilitate access for disabled people to education, training and personal development.

National Federation of the Blind of the UK

Sir John Wilson House, 215 Kirkgate, Wakefield, West Yorkshire, WF1 1JG
Tel: 01924 291313
www.nfbuk.org
Organisation to make life easier for blind/partially blind people.

National Handwriting Association

www.nha-handwriting.org.uk
The National Handwriting Association is a charity whose aim is to raise awareness of the importance of handwriting as a vital component of literacy.

Network 81

10 Boleyn Way, West Clacton, Essex, CO15 2NJ
Tel: 0845 077 4055
www.network81.org
This national network of parents advises parents about special needs provision and statementing.

NFER-NELSON (now GL Assessment)

9th Floor East, 389 Chiswick High Road, London, W4 4AL
Tel: 020 8996 8445
www.gl-assessment.co.uk
Provides specialist resources and testing equipment for special needs.

Pearson Assessment

Halley Court, Jordan Hill, Oxford, OX2 8EJ (customer services)
Tel: 0845 6308888 (8.00am - 5.00pm, Monday to Friday)
info@psychcorp.co.uk
www.psychcorp.co.uk

Penfriend XP LTD

30 South Oswald Road, Edinburgh, EH9 2HG
Tel: 0131 668 2000
www.penfriend.biz
Penfriend software benefits users who have dyslexia, visual impairment or physical disabilities and any condition which impairs the ability to write with a keyboard.

Portage Service (National Portage Association)

Kings Court, 17 School Road, Hall Green, Birmingham, B28 8JG
www.portage.org.uk
Portage is a home-visiting educational service for pre-school children with additional support needs and their families.

Pre-School Learning Alliance (formerly Playgroup Association)

The Fitzpatrick Building, 188 York Way, London, N7 9AD
Tel: 020 7697 2500
www.pre-school.org.uk
This national educational charity advises about pre-school and education.

Psychological Corporation (now part of Pearson Assessment)

Halley Court, Jordan Hill, Oxford, OX2 8EJ
Tel: 0845 630 8888
www.psychcorp.co.uk
Catalogue for specialist testing for educational psychologists, schools, etc.

REM

Great Western House, Langport, Somerset, TA10 9YU
Tel: 01458 254 700
www.r-e-m.co.uk/rem
Leading independent supplier of educational software.

Royal College of Speech and Language Therapists

2 White Hart Yard, London, SE1 1NX
Tel: 020 7378 1200
www.rcslt.org

RNIB (Royal National Institute for the Blind)

105 Judd Street, London, WC1H 9NE
Tel: 0303 123 9999
www.rnib.org.uk
Leading charity working for blind and partially-sighted people.

SEMERC

Angel House, Sherston, Malmesbury, Wiltshire, SN16 0LH
Tel: 0800 258 5991
www.semerc.com

SEN Legal

Units 3-4, Forbes Business Centre, Kempson Way, Bury St Edmunds, IP32 7AR
Tel: 01284 723952
www.senlegal.co.uk
Legal firm specialising in education law and special needs.

SEN Marketing

618 Leeds Road, Outerwood, Wakefield, WF1 2LT
Tel: 01924 871697
www.senbooks.co.uk
Specialist software catalogue available.

SKILL

4th Floor, Chapter House, 18-20 Crucifix Lane, London, SE1 3JW
Tel: 020 7450 0620
Info Line: 0800 328 5050
www.skill.org.uk
National Bureau for students with disabilities in post-16 education, promoting opportunities in training and employment across the UK.

Society for Italic Handwriting (SIH)

Nick Caulkin, 203 Dyas Avenue, Great Barr, Birmingham B42 1HN
Tel: 0121 244 8006 (evenings/weekends only)
www.nickthenibs.co.uk/calligraphy.htm
nickthenibs@hotmail.co.uk

Book List

Alternative Therapies

Dyslexia and Alternative Therapies
By Maria Chivers, JKP Essentials

ADHD

ADHD, Research, Practice and Opinion
Edited by Paul Cooper and Katherine Bilton, University of Cambridge.

Hyperactive Child
By Belinda Barnes, Foresight, £5.95.

Dyslexia

Adult Dyslexia: Assessment, Counselling and Training
By David McLoughlin, Gary Fitzgibbon and Vivienne Young, WHURR.

Brian Has Dyslexia – A Dr Spot Case Book
By Jenny Leigh, Red Kite Books.
Helps explain to very young children what dyslexia is.

Catch 'em Young
By Judith Stansfield.

Dealing with Dyslexia
By Pat Heaton and Patrick Winterson, WHURR.

Dyslexia a Hundred Years On
By TR Miles and Elaine Miles, Open University Press.

Dyslexia: An Introductory Guide
By James Doyle, WHURR.

Dyslexia and Alternative Therapies
By Maria Chivers, JKP Essentials

Dyslexia and Other Learning Difficulties – A Parent's Guide
By Maria Chivers, Need2Know.

Dyslexia, Dyspraxia and Mathematics
By Dorian Yeo, Emerson House, London.

Dyslexia, Speech and Language: A Practitioner's Handbook
Edited by Margaret Snowling and Joy Stackhouse, WHURR.

Dyslexia at College
Liz Du Pre, Dorothy Gilroy and T.R.Miles Routledge (New edition 2007t)

Dyslexia, The Inner Hurt
Edited by Maria Chivers, Forward Press, 1995.

Every Letter Counts
By Susan Hampshire, Bantam Books,1990.

Growing Up With Dyslexia
By Margaret Newton, NAMCW.

How to Detect and Manage Dyslexia
By Philomena Ott.

How Dyslexics Learn Grasping the Nettle
By Dr Kate Saunders and Annie White, PATOSS.

Introduction to Dyslexia
By Lindsay Peer and Gavin Reid.

Overcoming Dyslexia
By Dr. Beve Hornsby, Macdonald & Co, London.

Practical Strategies for Living with Dyslexia
By Maria Chivers, Jessica Kingsley.

Dyslexia and Stress
T.R.Miles & V.Varma (Eds) Whurr 2004

Susan's Story
By Susan Hampshire, Bantam Press.

Tackling Dyslexia
By Ann Cooke, WHURR, 2002.

Teaching Reading and Spelling to Dyslexic Children
Margaret Walton David Fulton Publishers 1998

The Gift of Dyslexia
By Ronald Davis and Eldon Braun.

This Book Doesn't Make Sense
By Jean Augur, Better Books & Software Ltd.

Understanding Dyslexia
By TR Miles.

Dyspraxia

Developmental Dyspraxia
By Madeleine Portwood, David Fulton. A practical manual for parents and professionals.

Dyspraxia: The Hidden Handicap
By Dr Amanda Kirby, Souvenir Press.

Living with Dyspraxia – A Guide for Adults
By Mary Colley.

Praxis Makes Perfect 11
A Dyspraxia Foundation publication, an essential guide for parents and teachers.

Dyscalculia

Butterworth B
Dyscalculia screener, Nfer-nelson, 2003.

Maths for the Dyslexic: a Practical Guide
Anne Henderson David Fulton Pubs 1998

The Mathematical Brain or "What Counts" (US version)
by Brian Butterworth.

Dyscalculia: Action Plans for Successful Learning in Mathematicsby Glynis Hannell. (2005)
David Fulton Publishers Ltd, London

Mathematics for Dyslexics including Dyscalculia
by Steve Chinn and Richard Ashcroft. (2007, 3rd Edn). John Wiley & Sons Ltd, Chichester.

Teaching Mathematics to Students With Learning Disabilities
by Nancy S. Bley & Carol Thornton. (2001)

The Trouble with Maths: A Practical Guide to Helping Learners with Numeracy Difficulties
by Steve Chinn. (2004). Routledge Falmer, London.

Mathematics for Dyslexics – A Teaching Handbook
By S Chin & R Ashcroft, WHURR.

Mathematics Solutions – An Introduction to Dyscalculia
By Jan Poustie et al, Next Generation. Teaching tips and resources.

Steps Ahead in Dyscalculia
By Cowell & Chivers, 2009. This is the workbook to go with the Steps Ahead in Dyscalculia Scheme also by Cowell & Chivers. The Scheme also has a dyscalculia test; details can be found online at www.dyslexiaa2z.com.

Dysgraphia

Dysgraphia and Other Learning Difficulties – A Parent's Guide
By Maria Chivers, DyslexiaA2Z.com.

Handwriting Rescue Kit
By Pippa Chudley, REM.

Handwriting Without Tears
By Molly Shannon, OTR/L., Harcourt Assessment.

Why Johnny Can't Write
By Diane Walton, Cavey Pub, Pro Ed. A handbook for teachers and parents.

Education Otherwise

Home Education & The Law
By David Deutsch and Kolya Wolf, 19 New Cross Road, Oxford, OX3 8LP.

Giftedness

Assessing Gifted and Talented Children
By Carolyn Richardson, The Qualifications and Curriculum Authority.

Working with gifted and talented children: Key Stages 1 and 2 English and mathematics
Contact QCA publications on 01787 884444.

CPSIA information can be obtained
at www.ICGtesting.com
Printed in the USA
LVOW04s1617190917
549279LV00002B/4/P